GIGS:

A Beginner's Guide to Playing Music Jobs

GIGS:

A Beginner's Guide to Playing Music Jobs

Sharon Black

Illustrated by the author

Edited by Brigid Rafferty
Benny Publishing
Skokie, Illinois

Publisher's Cataloging-in-Publication
(Provided by Quality Books, Inc.)

Black, Sharon (Sharon P.)
  gigs: a beginner's guide to playing
music jobs / Sharon Black ; illustrated by the author ;
edited by Brigid Rafferty. - - 3rd ed.
  p. cm.
  Includes index.
  LCCN 2007931712
  ISBN 978-0-9674813-2-6

  1. Music--Vocational guidance. I. Rafferty,
Brigid. II. Title.

ML3795.B59 2002   780'.23'73
                       QBI02-620

Acknowledgments

Special thanks to Diane Alison, Mark Amenta, David Bean, Nancy Christopher, Eugene Kwok, Mid West Talent/North Shore Pianists, Betty Monahan, Gail Petravick, Jennifer and Alan Swain, Cindy Tenney -Fudala, Vishal Vaid and Anna and Ernesto Valenzuela. Published with the permission of World Bible Publishers, Inc. Iowa Falls, IA 50126, U.S.A. for definitions on pages 12, 29, 64, 84, 138, 148, 171, 188 and 192.

Dedication

To my parents,
without whom there would be no gigs,
and to my husband,
without whom there would be no Gigs.

TABLE OF CONTENTS

A note from the start

Dear Readers,

    I hope GIGS will be a friend you can consult about your music life. Often, the pronoun "his" or "her" is used, and is meant to include either gender. It is useful to know that although names have been changed, **every story and cartoon is true, or nearly so.**

                                                    S.B.

Introduction
WELCOME TO GIGS 101

Welcome to GIGS 101! You're joining a class with amateurs who want to become professionals, up-and-coming musicians who need a little help and advice, and working musicians who need a fresh outlook and some polish. Meet four members of the class:

Baby Gigger (B.G.) is a budding musician who knows 18 songs. She doesn't have business cards yet.

Georgia Ballanchain is a talented singer/pianist who has been working off and on. But there's always an obstacle slowing her down!

Benny is a performer and a music teacher. We're not exactly sure what he plays, but he's really into it!

Boomer is Benny's right-hand man. He's worked for years, but he's here for some fine-tuning.

So, class, what are you here for?

We want to work!

Great! Let's start out by discussing what comes before work.... practicing!

Chapter One
PRACTICING

What is practicing?

Practicing means more than fingering an instrument. For a professional musician, practicing includes the following:

- LISTENING to music
- DECIDING what needs to be learned
- ACQUIRING the materials needed to learn the piece and
- CONCENTRATING completely when working.

Effective practicing comes from having specific daily and weekly
goals and striving for **no wasted time**.

One problem in practicing is that musicians don't know they are
making mistakes. In this case, the musician needs an authority to point
out the problem. An authority isn't only a person—see the list below:

- The score: if you play a piece continually from memory, it can become inaccurate. Check the written notes periodically.
- A metronome: this instrument will help you detect the problem measures. Practice the isolated measures at slower speeds until they catch
up to the rest of the piece.

- Recordings: these often teach the meaning or mood of a piece. Carefully studying the words will help you decide what the tempo should be.
- Second opinions: try pieces out on your friends or teachers and listen to their suggestions.

Musicians need to constantly be on guard against a wandering mind. If it is a challenge to concentrate fully, practice in five and 10-minute segments with a timer. Give yourself an allotted time for each musical task. The timer will jolt you out of any daydreaming.

We all need to warm up technically, right? Consider that the ear and the mind also need to warm up. If you plan to learn a new tune, begin your practice session by listening to either that piece or one in the same style. Fill your ear with the type of sounds you plan to make.

If you have a habit of practicing with your eyes on your instrument, try playing with closed eyes. This method improves concentration and helps memorization. You'll gain a freedom that will allow you to look up and extend more eye contact to your audience.

Musicians with varied practicing habits are enrolled in Gigs 101.

"I practice three hours a day! With all of this effort, why don't people contact me?"

Professional musicians practice with jobs in mind. Your professional time needs to include searching for and finding work. This activity will be discussed in Contacts, Chapter Three.

"Practice this stuff, are you kidding? I've got two degrees! Funny, though. I get plenty of first-time bookings, but they never ask me back."

Degreed musicians are not necessarily convincing performers of non-classical music. It is crucial to spend time listening to recordings and carefully choosing music for select audiences.

"I only have 45 minutes daily to practice, and 15 minutes of it is spent on making and keeping contacts. But it's working and I'm working."

It sounds like this person carefully plans how to spend 30 minutes of practice time.

Practicing with specific goals

Let's hope you have only a limited amount of time to practice—if you have all afternoon, you won't get a thing done! Don't vaguely charge at your instrument. Instead, write a specific list beforehand of what you need to do in a period of 30 to 45 minutes.

I have 45 minutes.
The first 5 minutes
are spent planning.

Read Benny's practicing plan below. He changes the actual pieces frequently, but his plan stays the same.

Benny's plan:

5 minutes	writing down practice goals and assembling music
15 minutes	technical warm-up
10 minutes	music for his current steady gig, including one new piece and three small corrections from the night before
15 minutes	one long, ongoing piece, plus review of the difficult passages of one piece for a new demo he's planning to make in six months

About the corrections: they were small, tedious ones, but Benny "made a note of them" as soon as they appeared during his playing job. He briefly stopped after the song and jotted down the name of the piece and its problem to be corrected during the next day's practice session.

It looks like B.G. has found a place to perform.

I'm going to play in a coffee house in a month. I have to get home and start practicing!

Hold it! Practice EFFECTIVELY by first planning out what needs to be done. What is your objective?

They told me to play a 45-minute set, and I want to know two new songs by then.

Before charging at your instrument, outline your practice goals.

Hmm, this first week I need to work the hardest on the new tunes and decide for sure what I'll play. Then I'll get up my nerve and play the program all the way through.

Now that B.G. has goals in mind, she can plan out 45 minute practice sessions efficiently. Here's what a practice plan might be on a typical day in Week Two:

10 minutes	technical warm-up
10 minutes	newest pieces, especially memory work
15 minutes	program "tops and bottoms" (in other words, the beginning and ending of each piece) memorization work
10 minutes	some other project, such as a holiday song for a family party

It takes patience to plan an effective workout.

Yeah, it would be easier to rush around and get all stressed over it.

I'm gonna practice 2 new songs before bagel break.
Wait! Call the café and ask for an audition!
Now? I was going to call them in the afternoon.
DON'T DELAY
Hello, could I speak with ... blab, blab ... you can see me tomorrow?
That changes it! I have to spend this time on the audition songs!

No monotony

Practicing should NEVER be boring or mindless. Be alert and focused on what you are trying to achieve, literally every minute. If you are playing scales, for example, you are listening for qualities such as accuracy, balance, evenness and speed.

 Benny and I get bored practicing the same tunes, but we need to do it anyway.

You aren't supposed to practice the same improvement over and over again. Every time you practice a particular piece, look for a new goal to achieve. Don't even think of the name of the tune. Say instead, "We're tightening up the endings today," or "We're changing the key."

Okay, today I'm focusing on the tempo changes, and Benny will be transposing the last chorus.

Practice time includes old repertoire. If you are bored with an old tune, find something in it to improve in order to make it fresh. (It may feel new again if you combine it with another song, too.) Listen to a recording of it. While you listen, examine (or re-examine) the following components of the piece:

tempo, bass line, melodic climax, chords and harmony, meaning of the words and technical sections.

If you continually find something NEW to bring out, drudgery will have no place in practice time. Make it a regular habit to correct the measures you think no one notices ... or read on to the advertisement on the next page.

Have GOALS in your practicing, for the day, the week, for your next performance and for the future. If you write a list and check it afterward, you'll know that you used your time efficiently.

Chapter Two:
CONTACTS

How do you make your contacts?

In other words, how does a musician find contacts for jobs? Music work comes in on different avenues including:

Contacting establishments and other sources who don't know you. This includes cold calls, mailings and ads.

Milking the most out of your present job. This means doing things in your current musical activities that will bring in work.

Places and people call YOU because they have heard you or heard *of* you.

What, no expressway?

How do you guys get your contacts?

I say yes any-time somebody needs music.

I try anything that will improve my playing.

Contacts come by meeting people through performance. It isn't quantity (like sending out 200 mailings) that brings in work. It often is doing the little things that are scary, like making a quick left turn into a banquet hall when you happen to be all dressed up, then introducing yourself to the manager.

Forget it!

It is sitting down after a job and writing a few thank you notes. It is following through with the ideas that keep occurring to you. But no, you don't want or need to contact every entity on the Internet.

Who needs your services? Start with people literally in your path. Musicians, you are not trying to GET something; you have valuables to offer!

But there's so much competition out there!

There is? When someone needs an accompanist, a last-minute entertainment or a holiday act, she feels as though there's NOBODY out there. She wants her need filled, fast, and doesn't want an army of appli-cants either. Often a musician is hired to work immediately, ready or not.

Contacts change. The list of treasured contacts you may have now might soon be replaced by a new group. Here's Benny's current handful of work sources.

 Party Planner: She likes Benny's work and his prices. The planner calls Benny first because if he can't take the job, he recommends someone equally proficient.

 School Placement Office: Benny continually thanks his alma mater for giving his name out to inquirers.

 The File Box: Cards from musicians, caterers, entertainers and music teachers are always being added.

 Steady part-time gig: Benny prepared three months for this audition, and it was worth it. People often ask for his card and inquire about his availability for outside jobs.

 Families: Benny plays a few times a year for several large families who love music and entertain often. He was referred to them by private music teachers.

Keep in mind that Benny has been working as a professional for several years. Baby Gigger's (B.G.) contact list is considerably smaller:

 Private teacher: B.G.'s teacher is happy to point out playing opportunities.

 School: This source includes friends, teachers and accessibility to the ad board that lists any need for musicians.

 Church: As a result of volunteering at holiday services, B.G. has been asked to play for a wedding.

Persons and places to contact

The following list is good for referrals:

- school placement offices
- wedding stores
- caterers
- agents
- party planners
- music teachers
- local musicians
- music stores

Great for holiday events:

- businesses
- corporations
- institutions

Read these:

- want ads
- dining guides
- job placement boards
- society pages

Places to perform:

- community theaters
- banquet rooms
- school theater departments
- retirement complexes
- low-budget television shows
- churches
- college faculty parties
- country clubs
- department stores
- farmers markets
- malls
- nursing homes
- eating and drinking establishments
- open mike nights
- hotels
- resorts

The best way to contact an establishment is to introduce yourself to the manager. In the beginning, the hardest part is using good old-fashioned courage. After you lose all fear of approaching people, the effort lies in taking the time to stop and do it. Make it a routine to stop at one place after each gig. *Minutes of effort speaking in person can equal hours and money spent on mailings and cold contacts.*

I dread introducing myself to someone and asking for work.

You are NOT asking a favor of the manager. You are offering something of value to the establishment. The manager is just a friendly bridge to the people your music will serve.

Sometimes it IS effective to send out mailings. Try this idea:

Pick ONE major business (insurance companies, for example) and contact each one in your area. If you are aiming for holiday parties, approach these organizations in early September. Send your letter or card to an appropriate name and finish the task with a follow-up call one week later.

Example: During a slow week in August, Ron, a composer / pianist, contacted more than 200 medical groups headquartered in his area. So many prospects called that Ron booked up his December calendar. He kept these contacts in his file for the following year.

Contact institutions that need your unique services. For instance, a Hispanic organization hosting an annual scholarship awards luncheon might be interested in a mariachi band. A department store presenting a spring focus would want light and carefree music, such as a Jamaican music combo.

Keep a "Tickler File" of places or people who should hear from you periodically. This list especially includes other musicians who could refer jobs to you. Send these persons new cards, brochures, clippings, pictures or news, and keep a record of what you mailed. Sometimes people receive your information and call immediately … other times, they may save it and call you when their daughter gets engaged six years later.

Tell your teacher (if you have one).

Alfreda has a performance degree in sackbut and has been asked four times to play at weddings. (Everybody wants a sackbut at his wedding, right?) But she never told her teacher or asked for help. Why? Because she was embarrassed; afraid of what her teacher would think of her attempting to play professionally so soon, and afraid to let the teacher know she was competing for jobs.

Tell your teacher! It benefits your teacher to help you. By helping you with your ambitions he becomes a better educator. The teacher raises his status by having a student who is a professional. Finally, the teacher will eventually gain you as a trusted substitute or referral.

Is this what my brother meant when he used to call me a sackbut?

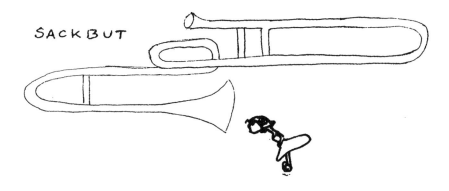

SACKBUT

Contacts? Tell me about it! To get work you have to know somebody!

I made a jingle recording but you have to know someone and I don't know anybody.

Have you heard comments like these before? To advance, you do have to know someone... yourself. You are a person without a lazy bone in your body. You are not a complainer. You do not fret unnecessarily in your speech or slump in your posture. You are happy for any opportunity to share your talents!

25

Phone skills

It's time to take out the local dining guide. When you begin calling places, don't be surprised if you make 30 or 40 calls before gaining one prospect. The conversations below are real, made by a novice musician, once upon a time.

Call #1 *You won't believe this call* .
"Hello."
"Hi (stammer) uh, I'm a classical guitarist looking for a place to play."
"What?"
"I-I'm a guitar player looking for a place to play."
"Vee no have music here." Click.

Call #9 *Finally he started asking for the manager.*
"Shamrocks."
"Hello, could you tell me the name of your manager?"
"Pat."
"Is he in right now?"
"It's a she." Click.

Call #19 *Avoid meal hours!*
"Hotel Sun."
"Hello, could you please tell me the name of your manager?"
"This is the manager speaking."
"Oh, hi, my name is Phil S. I'm a local musician and I'd like
 to know if you have any live music at the pool."
"We used to. Are you playing anywhere?"
"Duh, buh, I ..." Click.

Note: It helps to speak on the telephone with a big smile on your face.
This actually lifts the tone of your voice and makes you sound better.

Call #27 *They don't need to know that your job is a volunteer one.*
"George's."
"Yes, may I speak with George, please?"
"This is."
"George, hello, I am a classical guitarist performing at the Tall Oaks right now. I noticed your brunch ad and would like to come in and audition for you."
"Sure, come in around two o'clock."

It's really difficult for me to make these contact calls.	RING! There's the phone. Hello?
	Excuse me, that was some salesperson.

Many opportunities are lost because of a lack of professionalism on the phone. The following call is being made by Quincy, who needs better phone skills. He has an informative History of Musical Comedy presentation to offer schools and retirement groups. He is calling a retirement residence, which has been contacted already, to find out where it is located.

Seasons: Hello, this is the Seasons, can I help you?

Quincy: Would you tell me the crossroad you're on?

Seasons: W-What?

Quincy: What crossroad are you on? I just want to drop something off.

Stop, go back. At least start with "Good morning, would you please tell me the name of the crossroad the Seasons is on?" If there is any question, introduce yourself and state your purpose.

Seasons: What company are you representing?

Quincy: Is the manager there?

No, answer her question! You are a musician offering the Seasons a presentation called the History of Musical Comedy and you need to leave some information concerning your program.

Seasons: (annoyed) I am the Assistant Manager.

Quincy: I talked to the other manager already. Do you have a piece of paper, could you write a message?

You sound condescending; of course she has a piece of paper. You still need to introduce yourself.

Seasons: What is your name? (He tells her.)

Seasons: I would not consider hiring you. Good-bye.

Quincy: What's HER problem?

Quincy, be more formal in your speech and politely and accurately answer all questions.

Milking the cow for all she's worth

Wherever you are right now, your situation may be loaded with opportunities for musical sharing and improvement. Are you squeezing the full value out of every musical experience? Answer the following questions:

Am I ...
- performing for SOMEBODY on a regular basis?
- working on any ideas that really excite me, such as composing, recording, seminars, contests or recitals? (Any of these activities can lead to better work.)
- keeping a resume, brochure or social-networking site current?
- practicing regularly?

In steady and single gigs, am I ...
- striving for new ways to improve on the job?
- learning specific tunes for customers or staff?
- giving out cards, smiles and information? (Note: If you are playing in an ensemble, it is customary to give out only the leader's card and refer all jobs to the leader.)

Don't drive, STRIVE to work today!

strive, *v.*
1. **to make great efforts; try very hard.**
2. **to struggle.**

Getting back to "milking the gig," here's a list of things to do at a one -time job to help this gig multiply into more jobs:

- Write on your copy of the contract all of the highs and lows of the event and your own performance.
- Follow up on anything that could have improved the gig.
- Send a reminder for the next party.
- Ask the host, or even a very enthusiastic guest, if you can use his name for a reference.
- Speak with the manager at an unhectic time.
- Follow up with the manager by mail or phone.
- Thank your referral, if there is one.
- Thank your host in writing.

Please, not
anudder thing.

Hold it! You're talking about milking on the job? I don't have any jobs! I've never had any gigs before!

You've probably been sharing your music all of your life. Now you are ready to offer it in a more professional, expansive way. Start with the goal of being MUSICALLY ACTIVE. Count any musical performance as a job and treat it seriously.

When you DO have work, treat the job or contacts with great appreciation. If a particular office or person regularly recommends you, pay a friendly call with a small gift or sincere thank you. Appreciation is sometimes expressed through commissions or gifts, and always lots of thank you calls, notes or e-mails. Help these same contacts by subbing on a moment's notice, recommending competent musicians when you can't take a job and being prompt, loyal and positive.

Don't rely solely on old contacts, however. As with your repertoire, you need to be continually adding to your list, at least until you are satisfied with your amount of work.

Making contacts can be as much fun as performing. Would you enjoy adding your music to an hour of beauty, glitz and the wedding biz? Eric, a string player, volunteered to play for a luncheon preceding a fashion show as a way to contact brides and offer cards. What came of it? Amusingly, no weddings! While there, he was invited to eat and converse with some top magazine editors. The manager of the hotel was very interested and offered work. Even better, one bride gave Eric's card to a party planner who became a valuable work source for years.

Chapter Three:
BOOKING A SINGLE GIG

When they call you

To book an event means to engage it ahead of time. Some events are booked years in advance, while others are offered the day before.

ring!

My contacts are starting to call me!

The person calling you needs to hear your enthusiasm and eagerness to serve his needs from the very beginning. He will probably volunteer much of the information you need about the event. If the caller says, "I was just calling to find out how much you would charge for an hour or two," you may not want to quote a set rate without knowing more information. Ask questions like these:

- *Have you selected a date and location yet?*
- *Is there a particular type of music you're looking for?*

When the job is certain, you should learn more details:

- *Is this party a special occasion?*

31

- *Could you describe the room where the music will be played?* (This may determine whether you need amplification or not.)
- *What are the names of the honorees?*
- *Is the attire formal or casual?*

Of course, your contract includes the basic information such as time, location, fee, etc. (Contracts will be discussed later.)

If someone calls to inquire and says he or she will call back in a few days, follow up immediately with an email or brochure and some information. This shows you are dependable and interested. You are NOT being pushy—people want to make this decision as quickly as possible, and your information helps them decide.

 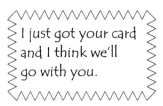

Confirm the event three to five days ahead. This is reassuring to the host and helps both sides approach the event with happy anticipation.

Here are two sample booking calls:

Call #1

Hostess: Hi, is this the harp player? I've been saving your ad from the *Review* for six months. I'm having an anniversary dinner for my parents and we want some background music. Do you do anything like that?

Harpist: I sure do. Would you tell me the date you have in mind?

Hostess: February 23, probably around 6:30.

Harpist (checks calendar): That's open! Is there a particular kind of music you were thinking about?

Hostess: We really like the show tunes. (She names a current show.) Maybe a little classical music during dinner.

Harpist: I just saw that show! How many people are you expecting?

Hostess: About 50. Mostly family members and some children, too.

Harpist: My students have taught me plenty of kids' songs.

Hostess: What would you charge for something like this?

Harpist: I normally charge ___ for three hours, depending on how far away the party is. (She names a fee.)

Hostess: It's at our home in Pine Hills.

Harpist: That's not far.

Hostess: Is there anywhere we could come to hear you?

Harpist: Whenever someone calls, I usually play a little over the phone! Could I play for you for two minutes?

Hostess: Uh … well … go ahead!

(Harpist plays three well-rehearsed excerpts from a jazz standard, a classical piece and a show tune.)

Hostess: That sounded wonderful.

Harpist: Well, thanks! I just wanted you to hear some music right away.

Hostess: It sure saves a lot of time for me. (Pause.)

Hostess: Well, I'd like to have you come. Do you need to come early to set up?

Harpist: Yes, by 6:15. I'll need to ask you a few things. (Musician fills out the contract information including name, address and phone, day and time, payment, etc.) I'll be sending you a contract to sign. Could you send it back with a deposit?

Hostess: Yes.

Harpist: It sounds like a great party. I'll send this out right away. Thanks for calling!

Hearing the music immediately reassures the caller. She can go back to family members or employees and say she has already heard you play.

GIVE THE CALLER YOUR UNDIVIDED ATTENTION

CALL #2

Banker: Hi, I was calling to find out what you would charge for some music. Our bank is honoring the local business of the year, Sicily Bread. The theme is Italian, so we need some Italian music, too.

Sax player: Could you first tell me the date so I could check my calendar?

Banker: September 9, probably from 4:00 until 7:00.

Sax (Checks date): I normally work with a keyboard player.

Banker: Do you play jazz?

Sax: Yes, lots of jazz standards, and the keyboardist plays boogie-woogie and ragtime. We can mix it in with some Italian songs.

(Sax knows jazz is a very broad field, and he is careful to be sure his list satisfies the caller. He knows they could NOT play a whole evening of improvisation, but that is not necessarily what the customer wants, anyway.)

Banker: Is it just the two of you?

Sax: We can add a bass player, or a drummer for dancing.

Banker: There won't be any dancing. What would be the charge for two or three pieces?

(Sax names a charge from his list of prices. He asks questions to find out more about the party and what the customer needs.) How many people are you expecting?

Banker: About 150. It's in our bank here. Can you bring a keyboard?

Sax: I need to check and see if my pianist is available. Yes, he does have a portable keyboard and a microphone if you need it.

Banker: That would really help. Last time, no one could hear the speeches because the mike was so distorted. Can you send me a tape?

Sax: Sure. I can stop by and drop it off tomorrow on my lunch hour. (This sounds like a repeat client, so Sax wants to meet her in person. They set up a time to connect.) Thanks, I'll see you tomorrow. 'Bye!

If you have to refuse a job, keep the caller's name and number. Your own schedule could change and you might become available after all. You can also send him a card to have on hand for his next event.

Question from a combo leader:

A party planner called and asked my fee for an out-of-town New Year's Eve party. I really needed some time to consider it—did I want to drive that far, could I find the instrumentalists he wanted, and what would the extra charges be? I mumbled and said it would be double my usual charge. It's not that the charge was wrong; I just wasn't feeling confident when I said it. What should I have done?

Do not feel pressured into giving anyone an immediate answer. If you need time to collect your thoughts, ask the caller if you can call back within the hour (not the next day or next week).

Dos and Don'ts in booking:

DO return calls only during business hours unless the contact requests otherwise.

DO speak with the contract information in front of you so that all discussion is done with complete accuracy.

DON'T sound indifferent or wishy-washy about the job the caller is offering. If you have doubts about taking the job, tell the person you will call back. Do so promptly to state your decision.

Sometimes, as you begin catching larger fish, you may be tempted to stop feeding the smaller ones. But it is important to sound interested in the caller's event.

In this case, the caller probably needed to understand Georgia's rate. Georgia could have briefly explained that she charges a two-hour minimum because there is often waiting involved at a luncheon and the charge includes the extra preparation of rehearsal, etc. If she were interested in the event, she should have mentioned her website or offered to send a brochure about her musical services. Rather than the fee, it is best to keep the call focused on the type of entertainment the caller needs.

Here goes...I have to remember to smile.	You're having a party? Let me check the date.
It's open! What kind of music do you like? Light pop? Let me try it!	Rock roll rattle shake
I'll send you a brochure today. Try to let me know by the weekend so that I can secure the other musicians.	JUST PRACTICING!

Tuning in

Sometimes a customer calls and goes on forever with details about the party. DON'T tune it out as useless chatter. The more you know, the better you can serve the event. Even before you're hired, jot down the details, including the type of occasion, who's invited and music the guests like.

But my repertoire is limited! I can't offer anything they want!

Expect to learn some new music for each single gig. (That's the best way to add to your repertoire.)

A singer called Jose to accompany her for a Top 40's party. They discovered that their repertoires were vastly different, but Jose was willing to try to learn a great deal of new material. After two rehearsals, the singer politely called it quits with him. The experience was an unfortunate loss of time, but a good lesson for Jose. He learned that if the job required tunes COMPLETELY out of his music field, it was wise to refer it to someone else.

Tune in to the caller!

Caller #1: The guests are a company branch of a national magazine and they...

Musician: (thinks) I don't need to hear all of this drivel! Why don't they just ask the price?

Tune in! A successful businessperson would only take the time to tell you something worthwhile.

Caller #2: "The people at this center are really hard to please."

Musician: (thinks) This lady is driving me crazy! I know everything is going to be fine, fine, fine!

Tune in. She's telling you something important about this group. Select your music with care.

Caller #3: "Our wedding is on the fourth of July weekend, so avoid Lake Shore Drive."

Read "Tuneout's Lament" in Weddings chapter.

Where could we could come to hear you?

Well, no, I'm not playing anywhere this month.

I don't want them to see the place I'm in this weekend.

Sure! I meet people at my teaching studio! Which would be best, a weekday or weekend?

You have several options besides inviting callers to a steady gig:

1. Perform over the phone. It's a pleasant surprise to the caller and very effective if your instrument is in tune and you have good acoustics in the room.
2. If you don't provide music on a website, send a tape. Follow up in a week to see if they received it. You may want to include an envelope that will enable them to return it right away.
3. Invite them over for an in-house consultation. This especially applies to wedding couples.
4. Give them some single gig dates to attend—the sooner the better.
5. Give them references, with the permission of your former hosts or employers.
6. For ensembles, invite the caller to a rehearsal.

Follow up each introductory call with a note of thanks and some information about yourself. This can greatly speed up the hiring process.

Referrals

You may wish to recommend another musician for the job. When you recommend someone, your own reputation is at stake. Be accurate with the caller and let him know if these are just strangers, or reliable persons you have actually heard or with whom you've worked. **Recommend musicians who you know to be professional in their speech, appearance and musical qualifications.**

When YOU come recommended or sub for someone, you are putting the other musician's reputation on the line. Make doubly sure that you are prompt and fulfill all expectations of the job.

Finally, go out of your way to thank whoever recommends you for a job. That person will feel appreciated and probably do it again. The words THANK YOU are downright melodious.

Anna auditioned a musician for the purpose of being able to recommend him for subbing. He was an average player and could sing. Anna recommended his services to a woman having a holiday party. To her surprise, the hostess called, ANGRY WITH HER, telling Anna what a mistake she had made. The guy had booked the party at a ridiculously low fee and later called saying that he had undervalued himself and raised his price! (That is a no-no. You must stay with the price you first mention.) The woman cancelled the job.

Then it happened again! Anna recommended an enthusiastic but inexperienced musician. The employer called her, very annoyed, telling her not to recommend him to anyone else because he spoke so discourteously over the phone. After this, Anna became extremely selective about referring names of other musicians.

Using a contract

Musician #1: I've never worked with a contract.
Musician #2: I've never worked without one.

A contract is a protection to both you and your employer. It will help your employer feel confident in you, protect you if an emergency arises, clear up miscommunications and give you a handy record of all your gigs.

A contract includes all necessary information about the job, such as date, location, hours, fee (including overtime) and deposit, as well as the signatures of both parties. If you are a member of a local union, you already use a standard form contract provided by the union. This book is not authorized to provide you any sample contract or tell you exactly what to put in it. Do have legal counsel for this important part of your business.

An entire group can lose a night's work when there is no contract and no correct address.

Don't just send contracts ... send a goody bag!

Remember that this event is very special to the caller. Let your personal note show that you are really looking forward to being there. Your host will enjoy telling guests where you play or study, as well as your other accomplishments. Include the following in your packet:

- contracts for you and the employer
- return envelope for your copy of the contract
- personal note
- business card
- brochure or news article
- photo (optional)

♪ Gigtime Story

One day while I was talking to another pianist, he reminded me of how we first met. I had arrived at a wedding reception to play on a grand piano, and he was already sitting there on the bench. In a mindless state, the mother of the bride had called him the day before, forgetting that another pianist had been contracted for months. The father was very apologetic. The question remained about who should stay and play. Contract to the rescue! I played, but the father paid us BOTH. (People feel pretty generous at weddings.)

At another banquet hall, the piano promised in the contract was already in use in another room. My concern was for the bride, who was so upset and angry. I showed them the contract and the careless management had to pay my fee and stick their heads in a Caesar Salad. (The bride felt better after that.) ♪

Chapter Four:
PAYMENT

What is payment?

Notice that the title of this chapter is not "Money." Money is not the only type of payment, nor is it necessarily the *best* payment. Before deciding how much to charge people for your services, it helps to know what payment really is.

WELL, WHAT IS IT ?!

Payment is compensation, and it comes in any of the following forms:

- fee or money
- barters or exchanges
- experience
- personal growth
- opportunities for more work
- gifts
- even enjoyment!

But the pay at my weekend gig is so low, it's humiliating.

Before you say the pay is too low, consider all of the ways you are receiving payment. Are you gaining experience? Is the job improving your musicianship or other areas of your career? Are you getting any fringe benefits? Do you enjoy the job? Does the job provide an opportunity to generate more work? A "yes" to any of these questions counts as payment.

I'm practically a full-time musician and while enjoyment is great, my payment has to cover the cost of my instrument, repairs, tapes and sheet music, as well as business costs such as the phone, office supplies and transportation.

The best way to raise your income is not to ask for a few more dollars per hour, but to use the steady job as an opportunity for more work. "Milk" the job and strive for contacts who will request your services for private gigs that pay more.

Bartering and partial bartering

Bartering is trading your goods for their goods. Have you ever thought about these opportunities?

- Playing for a [-$-] fee plus lodging at a vacation spot?

- Performing for a sum and a dinner gift certificate for two?

- Offering music in exchange for free classes or day care for your child?

- Playing in exchange for a [FREE TIX] material good?

These payments are often more valuable than a set fee—and more agreeable to the employer, too.

Deciding what to charge

When you start jobbing, it is difficult to know what to charge at first. New players generally charge lower fees than experienced musicians. Until they are able to provide the same level of professionalism, new musicians *should* charge less. Many people contact college music departments in hopes of hiring a good player at a low rate, so if you are in school or have a degree in ANY music area, let the placement office know you are available.

It helps to find out the rate other musicians are quoting. One way is to respond to music ads and inquire as any other customer would. Ask opinions of musicians you know; they may give you a tremendous variety of answers.

Some musicians charge by the hour. Musicians belonging to the American Federation of Musicians have set minimum wages. Others charge a flat rate for three hours and try to keep the gig lively enough to stretch into one hour of overtime. (Hosts are delighted to pay if it means that people are enjoying themselves so much, they don't want to leave!) For wedding ceremonies and shorter events, a two-hour minimum is appropriate.

Ensemble leaders add a leader fee to their charges to pay themselves for the extra time they spend on expenses, booking, organizing music and other time-consuming efforts. Some well-paid leaders take advantage of this arrangement by keeping a large percentage and paying their sidemen a measly sum.

BOO  HISS

Tipping is entirely up to the judgement and generosity of the host. Tip glasses are not used at private parties or receptions.

Carefully consider what your services are worth. Only experience will tell you how much extra to charge for travel time, bringing equipment or additional effort. If you are negotiating a steady job which pays on the low side, try compromising—four hours instead of five, dinner on the job, permission to have a substitute once a month, etc. If your jobs are scarce at the moment, reduce the fee and see what happens.

Remember: for one-time gigs, customers do not necessarily grab the entertainer with the lowest charge. They are more likely to hire the person who sounds the most interesting, as well as interested in them and their needs.

Most musicians quote a set price immediately; but if you are unsure of your fee, it is acceptable to tell the potential customer that you need to call back (in a few minutes) with the fee information. If a caller is critical of your fee, it is because he is only considering the time you spend at the event itself. Sometimes it is necessary to explain, especially to wedding couples, that the fee includes arriving early, rehearsal time and finding special pieces for the event.

 The man thinks he's paying me for 3 hours. But here's the work I'm really doing.

The work you are really doing includes the following:

- phone conversations with the customer
- written communication and contract writing
- planning the music with a specific audience in mind
- rehearsal
- additional time (getting directions, preparing attire, etc.)
- travel time
- arriving early
- THE GIG ITSELF
- unpacking at home
- thank you notes or calls

A three-hour gig means at least four hours of work, and in many cases it extends into much more. Are you worth what you are charging? If you are working to meet the above standards, you probably are. The musician who simply names a high fee without planning to provide the above services probably is not.

Beware of event planners who insist they only need music for 45 minutes.

Here is a sample of how a musician might determine his charges:

Wally has a trio that performs once a month for parties and wedding receptions. He currently charges $525.00 for a three-hour gig. Each player earns $150.00, and the remaining $75.00 covers the leader fee and expenses. Wally wants to know what other trios are charging, so he starts with the people he knows.

Experienced string player	$750
Wally's flutist with her own group	$525
Fellow musician	$750

He calls people who work as agents and charge a fee on top of the group's fee.

Party planner	$750- $900
Entertainment agency	$1,000

He researches gigs websites.

Dance band	$800
Classical trio	$900
Variety trio	$950

Wally can see that his rate is rock bottom. He also realizes that he deals largely with family parties, while the higher charges might be reserved for large companies. His rate was fine at first because his trio was just beginning, and sounded like it. Wally did not mind all of the extra hours he spent on the group, because any business owner would do the same. Now, however, he is in a position to charge more. He settles on $650 and increases his player's pay to $185, with $95 remaining for his own leader fee and expenses.

Hey, I'm self-employed! I can charge this way ...

$$

... or that way.

¢¢

Or this way

$$$$

or that way.

$ 0.00

What are you so charged up about?

51

Collecting your money

Most people who can afford your services are very responsible about payment. Nonetheless, here are a few "tips" for collectors.

Prevention

Word your contract to ensure that you receive a deposit at the time your services are booked, followed by the remaining payment in full on the day of the job. An employer should not object to this standard of payment. You shouldn't have to stand around waiting more than briefly for your money at the end of the gig.

When it is time to be paid, present your copy of the contract to show the employer the deposit he paid and the balance due. For a bride and groom, you might say, "I don't want to disturb you at the reception, so would it be possible for someone to give me the payment when I arrive?" Sometimes people want to pay in full ahead of time.

When something goes wrong

Occasionally, the host might say, "Just send me a bill," even though he has signed a contract saying he must pay on the day of the job. How often should you allow this? Almost never. Nicely remind the person, with your contract in hand, that you were to be paid on the day of the engagement. Smile and say, "Cash or check is fine!" If this is a good, steady customer, and you feel you must make an exception, prevent this situation from recurring by calling ahead next time to ask if the host needs your address or any other information for the check he will give you on the day of the gig.

But I'm afraid of what she'll think. I'm afraid of being a pain.

You aren't calling to be a pain, you are calling because you are happy, DELIGHTED to play for the job and you can't wait to be there! Your enthusiasm sets up a happy, positive atmosphere. And ... you want to be paid on time, that's all.

Super C, the man returned my contract, but he didn't include a deposit.

Call him.

I'm scared to call him.

You're being professional and helpful by clearing up a mistake.

I'm afraid of annoying or bothering him.

Pick a slow time, be brief and friendly.

But...I made the mistake of not talking about the deposit when he first called.

It is a good thing to mention.

Hi, Mr. Manager ?

It turned out that he wanted to send only one check, so he's mailing me payment in full ahead of time!

53

Overtime billing

Occasionally, you will have to submit a bill for your overtime work because the company printed your check ahead of time. It helps to keep appropriate stationery with you for this purpose—the company is happy if you can immediately present them with a simple bill. Sample:

Your name
address
phone

Entertainment services rendered on July 5, 2012
Total amount due: $350

If you bill by mail, enclosed a self- addressed envelope.
Send the overtime bill with a thank you note.

Receipts

Receipts are equally simple. If a customer requests one, you can write it yourself. Sample:

Your name here
Entertainment services provided on (date).
Payment received (fill in dollar amount).
Signed (your signature)

Or, buy a book of receipts at an office supply store.

Be helpful. Call the customer if you do not receive the payment within 10 days.

No inaccurate receipts

Benny had a hospital benefit scheduled. Upon confirming the gig, he discovered that the deposit and contract had not been returned. The hostess said she had mailed it days ago. The benefit day arrived and he still had not received the deposit. The hostess paid the remainder, and she and Benny agreed to wait one more week for the deposit to arrive by mail.

Here's the problem: she wanted a receipt in full. Benny said, "I'm sorry, I can't write an inaccurate receipt." She exclaimed, "Yes you can!" He even offered to delay all payment for one week if one receipt was what she needed, but he rightly refused to write an inaccurate receipt. The woman became mouthy and unmannerly, wrote a check for the complete amount in return for a receipt in full and plopped his coat down angrily for a good-bye.

Boo-hoo, she threw me down.

Please don't cry!

Benny felt uncomfortable about leaving the hostess in such a state, even though he knew he was right. He reviewed all of his actions in this unfortunate incident and realized several ways HE could better such a situation in the future:

- Be more systematic about opening mail. (The deposit MIGHT have been swallowed up with other papers.)
- Review the contract first before calling to confirm the job.
- Make a tally sheet to know all financial records at a glance.

As it turned out, the deposit DID arrive days later. Good job, Benny. You turned this problem into an opportunity to improve your own business.

If the very unusual happens and someone is totally irresponsible about payment, stay pleasant and PERSISTENT. Call the customer and call again and pay a friendly visit to collect. If that doesn't work, send registered letters until you get a response. Hopefully, bill collection will never have to go beyond this step. Avoid these mishaps by providing a contract, asking for a deposit and insisting on payment according to the contract.

Two case studies: A. Silligroom and D. Doughdad

At a megabucks reception, A.S. charmingly told the musician he couldn't pay that evening. Do you think that could be possible, with all those cash gifts on hand? After pleasant words were exchanged, his groomsmen took up a collection and paid the musician.

During a splendid prenuptial dinner, Doughdad came over just as speeches were beginning and whispered to the string player that he had forgotten his checkbook, "and I'm sure you don't take credit cards." He was very apologetic, but this error smacked of disrespect to the musical profession. The musician unhappily let it go, and to Doughdad's credit, he did mail the payment on the morning of the wedding.

i was called to accompany a singer / director in a show for a benefit.

```
. . . . . . . . . .
.                  .
.       ME         .
.      AND         .
.      MR.         .
.    NAUGHTY       .
.                  .
. . . . . . . . . .
```

the singer acted very oddly and irresponsibly from start.

I'm from a $$ family.

Since I don't have a car, would you drive me 5 miles to pick up some music?

this i learned:
   if you must gig for someone you have doubts about, word the contract so that you are paid in full before the job.

musically, he was great. he demanded the best efforts from both of us.

REPORT CARD	
name mr. naughty	
Expression	A
Dramatics	A
Musicianship	A+
Conduct	D

the show was a sort-of success and had plenty of cash-paying customers.

Not quite this: Just a few blemishes.

but mr. naughty wouldn't pay me even though i followed him around the cabaret for half an hour.

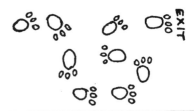

58

ahem, can anyone act deceitfully and truly benefit a cause?

?

i went home and called him, wrote cordial letters and contacted other show members for several weeks.

i was always pleasant and persistent. his friends said he stiffed them, too.

You were out while we called.

finally, i sent two registered letters — one to him and one to his landlord. soon after...

i remember that sweet moment of opening an envelope and seeing the right amount.

$

later, mr. n. asked me to accompany him again and also loan him my keyboard! he thought we'd worked so well together.

the end

59

Freebies

My Aunt Bigbucks told me never to play for nuthin'!

Yes, it certainly would be silly to perform for NOTHING. But are experience and fulfillment nothing? If you are an amateur, experience is what you most need. These situations have non-monetary purposes:

• Retirement homes: a retirement residence would be delighted with a musical volunteer. Ask for the social activities director and tell that person about the music you have to offer.

Gee, Granny and
her friends are
really enjoying this.

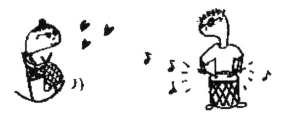

• Small scale television or radio shows

Look at what this
did for my resume!

• Low-wage restaurants

Soon I'll know 25
songs from memory!

The following columns show three biographies you might read in a play program. Many of the supposedly impressive credits are actually freebies (or nearly so).

☆ GEORGE CURI
(Musical Director)

This is George's debut as musical director for the City Players. In Atlanta, he provided music direction for a wide variety of musicals. He has also accompanied comedy revues at Zinger's. George has written more than twenty five original songs as well as incidental music for the award winning TV show, "Wildberry Tree".

—— could be school productions

—— very big name with very low budget

—— low-budget children's show

☆ JERRY PATEL
(Bassist)

Jerry is making his first appearance at the City Players. A string and electric bassist, he currently performs with the North Lake Symphony and the Richmond Symphony Orchestra.

—— no musical schooling

SUE LENNON
☆ *(Percussionist)*

This is Sue's second show with the company. She recently received a B.A. in Percussion Performance from State U., where she was active in both wind and jazz ensembles. Other performance experience includes The Contemporary Chamber Players and the Livingston Symphony Orchestra.

—— these may be volunteer groups

—— school activities

—— community groups

After reading between the lines, it's obvious that while these musicians are beginners in the field of musical theater, their credits and auditions earned them a professional show.

Speaking of freebies, people I hardly know ask me to sing at their weddings, for free! I resent this; they don't realize the work I am putting in.

The people who ask this favor of you are unaware of the effort and time it takes, let alone the other requests you receive. You need wedding business cards, and perhaps a written price list that stipulates that your price includes rehearsal time, consultation, music selection, early arrival and the performance. These materials let acquaintances know that as a professional musician, you are kept busy and cannot offer music as a gift except when appropriate. It may be best to have one standard response for everyone and treat all requests alike.

MUSICIANS HAVE TO BE CAREFUL ABOUT
VOLUNTEERING THEIR SERVICES.

Chapter Five:
ENRICHING THE EVENT

I have two
bookings this
month!

Georgia, this chapter is especially for you. It assumes you've worked for a little while and are ready to polish your skills.

Can I skip this?

Not so fast, Boomer.

Confidence

Be prepared to the best of your ability ... and then be confident, confident and confident! In yourself? Yes, in yourself AND everyone else at the event. You can be absolutely certain that every guest has something to contribute to the occasion. A gathering needs joke-tellers, talkers and people who listen appreciatively. It sure takes the pressure off to realize that everyone has something to offer.

But sometimes I have this feeling of dread, don't you?   No, I feel happy anticipation.

That sense of dread may come from inadequate preparation. Another feeling that crops up among musicians is the sense that they're cut off from the group they are performing for. As the "hired help," you're a stranger; yet you are supposed to offer warmth and life to the atmosphere.

The answer is to not think of your SELF or any self at all! Focus on the qualities your music adds to the surroundings. Fun, liveliness, tenderness, outrageousness … every song you play presents a quality of its own.

Aside from your contributions, what else contributes to the event's success ? All of the following items add something important:

- room and physical surroundings
- hired help, including party planners
- hosts and guests
- purpose or occasion
- edibles
- preparation

Staying aware of all of these factors should remove any sense of nervousness and replace it with anticipation.

Happiness is knowing that your music will enrich the event!

enrich, *v.*
1. to make rich.
2. to supply with anything splendid.
3. to decorate.
4. to add vitamins.

Assignment:
Put an X on every moving object that enriches.
Circle every still object that enriches.
Put everything else outside.

Packing for the gig

Georgia, are you packing the following for your gigs?

- **Clean instrument and equipment**: expect people to approach you; your work area must appear inviting.
- **Music picked specifically for the event**: consider carefully what the group would enjoy hearing.
- **List of your repertoire**: this is a lifesaver when you can't think of anything to ad lib.
- **Collection of very useful music**: your personal collection of "musical gems" will grow over time.
- **Cards, brochures and stationery**: display your card. Use a break to jot a note to the host or manager.
- **Contract**: always have it with you and be able to show your employer the payment that is owed.

Boomer, what
happened?

I think I passed out when I
heard, "clean equipment."

All packed, Georgia? There's just one more thing to remember. Bring your best in the departments of looks, language and habits. Ask the host about the dress code, if you are unsure of what to wear. Attire is important—even shoes should look appropriate and well-cared for.

Oh, come on!

The following are all true stories—and unfortunately common examples of musicians who left their professionalism at home.

- A bride was deeply offended (even years after her wedding) by a musician who sported a two-day old beard and a sloppy appearance.
- A talented singer/songwriter lost a valuable contact because his vocabulary (when he thought he was out of earshot) was so foul.
- One quartet member spilled a glass of red wine on crème draperies and carpet, losing any future bookings for the whole group.
- A string player was low on gigs because he didn't realize it was unmannerly to talk, laugh and be inattentive during ceremonies.

> Quite simply ...
> It is unprofessional
> to drink alcoholic beverages on the job.
> We are civilized and we sound like it.
> If we gig for a reception, party or ceremony,
> we dress and look our best,
> not to flaunt ourselves,
> but to honor the event.

Setting up

Setting up correctly is a key factor in making your music an important part of the event. Set up where the sound and guests' sight of you can immediately make an impact. If your act is moveable, it's an asset to begin performing at the entrance and welcome guests as they enter. (Hint: playing from memory makes eye contact easier.) If you and the guests communicate from the start (even with just a smile), this breaks the ice and makes you a friend who can comfortably visit with guests at tables later on. Having noticed the musicians from the start, the crowd is more likely to listen and respond as the event proceeds. Sometimes guests appear uncomfortable when they walk in. The musical atmosphere can help people to relax.

Generally, when people cluster around the food and beverages, the music needs to be near those areas. Also, the entire music area should look attractive—who wants to approach a messy, dusty set up?

Discuss with the host the time frame for toasts or presentations. Discourage piped-in music by saying, "My breaks are short, and it would be better not to turn on any other music." The room itself needs a breather which allows live music to be more appreciated when it resumes.

They're about an hour away by bus.

Avoid being placed rooms away from the refreshments.

♪ Gigtime Story

The hostess was detailed, pleasant and very firm. She told me my portable piano would fit nowhere but on the upstairs balcony, overlooking the entrance. Aah, a romantic balcony!

Upon arrival, I discovered the house to be large, seemingly spacious enough to accommodate the music downstairs or even outside. However, I set up in my appointed place. Suddenly, the door next to me swung open and out walked a man wearing only a towel—a small one. The hostess had placed me next to the bathroom.

This location turned out to be delightful for the guests' arrival. Soon, however, they all moved outside toward the pool. All I could do was sit around and awkwardly greet persons when they used the washroom. In the third hour, they came in and dined in a room far away from me.

Mid-evening, the hostess came upstairs, pleased with the tinkle of music she had been hearing, and paid ahead of time with a generous tip. Later, I received an exuberant thank-you note and an invite to come again next year.

Now, would you play that gig again? ♪

You call that a gig?

Mmm ... what type of magazines were in the washroom?

During the event

People throw parties for special occasions such as birthdays, anniversaries, holidays, graduation and pre-nuptial gatherings. Other occasions are more casual and involve neighbors, office workers or family. In any case, we musicians know that our art is a tremendous addition to the event!

If you are wondering what to play next, be observant and keep asking yourself, "What is needed here?" Music enhances what is already in the room. Think less about names of songs and more about the atmosphere you are helping to create.

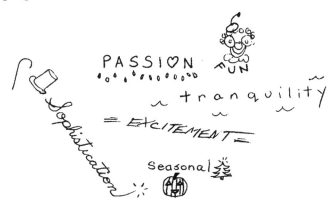

If you are performing in an ensemble and have a set program, be prepared to jump around to suit the party's flow. Keep balance in mind, too. Even if the requests are for one rowdy, high-powered tune after another, you'll need to give variety to the volume and energy for the sake of your repertoire and the other guests' sensibilities.

If you are a soloist, you can bring along books for people to browse through. Watch for extroverted guests and draw them out even further by communicating and playing their requests. They will draw out other guests.

If hours pass and you feel like you are playing one meaningless tune after another, it is time to stop and talk to someone. If people are seated, you can approach the host table. Congratulate the guest of honor, or ask people the type of music they would like to hear. (You are doing this to enrich the event, not to "make another sale." When people approach you for your card, give it out subtly and save money talk for the phone.)You might feel shy and want to avoid guests when you are on break. If this happens, firmly remind yourself of YOUR PURPOSE in being at this event. You are NOT a misfit; you are a perfect fit to the surroundings.

About eating: the host may or may not offer you a meal. If you are invited to eat, do so briefly on your break, generally apart from the guests.

Depending on the group, you may find that young adults pay the least amount of attention to the music. It's no wonder: they have experienced so much less of the type a live musician offers than their parents and grandparents have. If you don't play the music they favor, find music that appeals to this group, such as TV and movie themes, Grammy Award winning songs or classical and pop music they recognize. Remember: the young generations of today are our employers of tomorrow. It's worth accommodating them!

If this is a lively, fun affair, play anything you can that would please a guest, even the corniest and silliest of tunes. Be sure to play the host's requests at very obvious times (like when he's within earshot). Try to smile if the host announces, "Go ahead, ask her. She knows everything!" Also, a birthday and an anniversary song—don't leave home without them. Finally, at the end of the affair when the guests are lounging around and the hired help is dying to go home, you can play whatever you want!

Chapter Six:
PARTIES AND RECEPTIONS

The life of the party

As a one-time-in-history event, a party is really exciting! It doesn't have to be raucous to be successful. A party can have quiet or even awkward moments, yet still turn out fine. Your role at the party is that of a musical host. Depending on the occasion, you will be greeting, communicating, maybe announcing or advising; but most of all, you'll be filling the atmosphere with absolutely fabulous sound that you know is right for the room.

Just salting the
glass for tonight.

B.G., no! Tip glasses aren't
used for private functions.

Three Gigtime Stories:

♫ **The Misfortune**

One night, I performed at a ⟨plate⟩ dinner for a TV newsperson. Her young ⟨child's face⟩ daughter jumped up to dance during the ⟨fish⟩ salmon course. Total abandon caused her black ⟨shoe⟩ pump to fly into the air and miss my ⟨eye⟩ eye by an inch. It was so funny that I played while ⟨tear drops⟩ tears poured down my face. A video camera captured the whole scenario. Oh, such a ⟨mouth⟩ misfortune that the ⟨shoe⟩ shoe did not hit me! It would have surely won the $$$ prize on that home video TV show.

72

♪ The Privilege

Picture
A baroque drawing room

A baroque drawing room
With an eighteenth century keyboard

A baroque drawing room
With an eighteenth century keyboard
In a country estate on the lake

A baroque drawing room
With an eighteenth century keyboard
In a country estate on the lake
Visited by distinguished and gracious guests
Who dined in the bath house near the tennis courts.

Yup, gigs are a
privilege, alright.

♫ The Crash

Notes from A. Gigger

after a break it is nice to play something distinctive.	at a quiet company dinner in a ritzy hotel, a huge wooden soldier stood next to the piano.
he was the focal point of the christmas decor.	i returned from a break and began significantly with "parade of the wooden soldiers."
immediately, the soldier fell	and crashed to the floor. I'll be alright.

Feeling Ignored?

Sometimes gigs are a blast, and sometimes I wonder why I'm there at all.

Honestly, either you're playing in an empty room, or the crowd is so huge that you're utterly soundless! If providing background music is the gig, you have to deal with feeling like a human backdrop some of the time. If this happens, don't give in to boredom or depression. **You are there for a reason.** You are helping to create atmosphere both audibly and visually. The very moment you feel unappreciated may be the same instant that your music eases a tense situation unknown to you, or offers an icebreaker for many conversations.

Sometimes the employer wants the glamour of live music, but doesn't want it to detract from the speeches, food or gifts … until the last hour, when music suddenly becomes the focal point of the event.

There are gray areas between being ignored and being the center of attention. Think of the last time you walked into a room and were struck by the interesting wallpaper. Although you never examined it up close, it characterized the whole room and made an impression. Background music can make the same kind of contribution to an event.

Preventive measures to avoid being ignored:

- Set up in a location where people see you.
- If possible, move later to a different location.
- Take short breaks to walk around and be available to guests for comments and requests.
- Make the entire music area look inviting, with cards or brochures available to take.
- Smile and be friendly. People will be attracted to your warmth, even if they are not interested in the music.

Are **YOU** the one doing the ignoring by…

- Daydreaming?
- Practicing instead of performing? (It's great to try out tunes for future gigs, but always be alert to where you are.)
- Neglecting? Are you playing only to age groups with whom you feel comfortable?
- Wishing people would go home?

I see problems at parties, like bored guests or insistent hosts.

As the objective entertainer, you sometimes observe that the hostess is too insistent on having her own way, instead of going with the flow of the party. In the midst of any flaws you may notice, focus entirely on conveying the entertainment. Be confident that the music is adding a bright dimension, kind of like one great actor who saves a mediocre movie.

Last night was such a flop. Why does the host pay me all of this money and then have his guests hang out in the TV room?

Did ANYTHING good happen?

I did have some audience, mostly parents with small children who enjoyed the music.

In this case, think of the big-gig picture. You had one less-than-perfect party amid a year of many, many musical opportunities.

Strolling

Strolling is a wonderful way to project the music and avoid the problem of being ignored. Andrew was a string player and leader of a quartet that often booked wedding receptions. One time, however, he attended an affair as a guest. He noticed a string trio, which included an accordion, entertaining at the entrance without music. They seemed to be having such a good time. When everyone was seated, the trio strolled around the room playing familiar songs. One table exploded into singing, "Take Me Out to the Ball Game." The wedding guests at Andrew's table were disappointed when the strollers stopped and speeches began.

After watching these merry strollers, Andrew became painfully aware that his own ensemble, which generally sat in a corner with lots of sheet music, wasn't reaching the people. He realized that since his group had to remain seated, they at least needed to be highly visible and physically near to the guests.

Strolling is to an instrumentalist what sing-alongs are to a vocalist: a vehicle for sharing music. Gaining experience in this activity should overcome any feelings of self-consciousness.

Loud Talking

What do I do when talking drowns me out?

Instead of turning your volume up to the max, try these techniques:

- Play simple music with a simple melody.
- Play music with strong major or minor harmonies. Save the subtle minor sevenths for a quieter time.
- Think, "FULL." Keyboardists can play with big chords in octaves. Ensembles should choose arrangements with the fullest texture.
- Maintain a strong and a steady beat—one that people can feel even if they can't distinguish the tune.
- Ask someone if you can be heard. Guests may surprise you by saying they can hear the music across the room. The acoustics may have been on your side all along.
- Amplify your sound when necessary. Purchase a speaker and microphone, then have this investment pay off through more jobs.

Compliments

Sometimes you play for a party or reception and while people mill around, you feel unappreciated because no one speaks to you or compliments the music.

WHAT IS A COMPLIMENT? Take any reaction to the music as a compliment. Interpret any sign of life as a signal of the type of music to play. Notice guests walking to the music, doing a few dance steps, reacting with their hands, tapping feet, singing or saying the name of the tune to their friends. Once you start noticing *all* of the "compliments" you receive, verbal praise like "the music sounds great" will become less important.

SAFETY TIP	be alert! keep your eyes on your compliments at all times!

Feet:	Tapping
	Moving while legs are crossed
Legs:	Changing stride with the rhythm
Fingers:	Tapping on the arm of a chair or knees
	Wiggling
Eyes:	Staring
	Glancing
Bodies:	Carrying children and moving with them
	Dancing
Arms:	Conducting
Mouths:	Mentioning the music to their friends
	Talking to you
	Whistling
	Singing

IF YOU MISS THESE COMPLIMENTS, CONSIDER IT ROBBERY!

Is spitting
a compliment?

Not.

The best compliment is being invited back … again and again.

But I've already played my best stuff and I don't have an entirely new repertoire to offer.

You have proven yourself. Now, take a risk and try something new, depending on the crowd. Introduce a new musical activity that gets people involved such as:

1. **One special song performed for the honoree**. Change the words to suit the occasion.
2. **One page of songs honoring the occasion**. The host might write a script about that person's life, with the group singing intermittently.
3. **Sing-along with songbooks**. If you have already played sing-alongs with this group, add a new page to the front of the book.
4. **Limbo dance**, using a belt or tie for a limbo stick. Play appropriate music.
5. **Group dances**: Hokey Pokey, Chicken Dance, Bunny Hop, rhythms that inspire silly people to form a train.
6. **Ethnic**: Hebrew clapping songs, Hora, Mexican Hat Dance, etc.
7. **Children's games**: Farmer in the Dell, Bingo, Wheels on the Bus.
8. **Holiday:** "Twelve Days of Christmas" with new words. Give tables of guests different parts of the song to sing. Or, give one side of the room odd numbers and one side the even. Pick the best singer or the worst for the words "five gold rings."

Outdoor gigs

How lovely.

There's good:
- performing in a rock group onstage at Summerfest.
- playing the "Prince of Denmark" on trumpet for a glorious bridal procession.
- jamming with a Dixieland band on a boat.
- hearing your group blend with the sounds of nature.

There's bad:
- feeling like your fingers have frozen into an ice sculpture.
- having pages blow everywhere because nobody brought clips.
- watching your sweat actually drip onto the instrument.

And there's unsafe:
- losing an entire gig because the rain OUTSIDE the tent is so heavy that the ground is soaked and makes using the electrical equipment hazardous. (The gig might have been saved by bringing some back-up instruments.)

Outside gigs are only for the rugged! No guest could dream of how weather affects a musician's job. While the guests are delighted and the scene is sublime, outdoor musicians must take extra precautions to ensure that the job runs smoothly.

DO bring clips to all jobs. Even the slightest breeze can create havoc.
DO dress for the weather. There's nothing worse than freezing on a gig. (On the other hand, you may even need bug spray.)
DO prepare a thorough back-up plan in case of rain.
DO word your contract so that you perform in a dry, protected area.

Lucy's Outdoor Gig

Lucy was a harpist at an outdoor home wedding held on beautiful grounds. The setting was the height of refinement, which contrasted sharply with the guest list: ladies arrived dressed in camping attire and sporting large tattoos, while gentlemen approached Lucy to say things like, "Hey, like uh, who's dis?" While people wandered around, the host asked Lucy to play 40 minutes of prelude music, mostly classical. The breeze, as usual, was strong enough to blow the pages in her wedding repertoire book back and forth. Lucy knew that her only hope was to play entirely from memory, so she quickly wrote a list of all the possibilities. She was able to come up with 12 memorized pieces. While her performance didn't show all of her best repertoire, at least she didn't have to rely on sheet music. By the way, nobody heard the ceremony because of the wind. Lucy wished she'd brought a second microphone for da minister.

82

Chapter Seven:
I HOPE I GET

Attention, up-and-coming professionals: one of these days, someone may inform you that playing tunes is, well, a rather low occupation in music. Yessir, there are fancier cars in the lot! But nobody said that playing gigs has to be your only goal. Hasn't this book proven that "playing tunes" is a form of managing your own business? And that it's just plain fun? Let's move on and "get the gig."

Auditions

What is an audition?

audition, *n.*
1. a hearing
2. particularly, a hearing to test the abilities, voice, etc. of a speaker, actor or musician.

Every audition is a victory. You gain a job or you gain an experience. An audition is a wonderful opportunity to polish yourself and raise your skills a few notches.

Like the way annual houseguests are an opportunity to clean your apartment.

An audition is also an opportunity to network. Is an audition much different from a gig? It's a splendid opportunity to play your heart out and let others enjoy hearing you.

Hey, I'm guaranteed a good time!

Vincent was a highly confident music major from a small town. He graduated, moved to the city, and immediately called hotels to ask about

84

auditions. He met with a hotel manager and enthusiastically played for him for 20 minutes. To Vincent's surprise, he was not hired. He asked the manager the reason and the manager told him he played too much music in one style. Besides, the patrons of the hotel were largely older, successful business people, many visiting from other countries. More variety and well-known songs were needed.

If you experience a disappointment, ask the management the reason why. In this case, Vincent learned something valuable.

 I think you're forgetting I want the job! How about some tips?

Auditions usually mean performing your best repertoire for the manager or owner (often, with customers listening), as well as talking about the job and your own availability. Be prompt, dress in a way that you think is appropriate for the job setting (when in doubt, dress UP, not down) and arrive with a brochure or resume in hand. Unless you are accompanying a singer, play memorized pieces. The employer may ask you to provide a sample of your playing while he does other work nearby. At other auditions, several different listeners might ask for specific categories of music. They may even have a list of requests. In this case, it helps if you've brought some music along. Still, play from memory whenever possible.

If you are asked to play a song you don't know, act as you would on the gig. Happily offer an alternative by the same composer or a similar song from the same era. This response shows how relaxed and prepared you are if such a situation should arise.

What does the employer notice at your audition? Your ...

- musical skill
- choice of repertoire
- appearance and ease at the instrument
- communication abilities
- enthusiasm and attitude
- (in some cases) attire or costumes appropriate to the event

Questions an employer may ask:

- Where are you playing now? (If you don't have a steady position, you probably perform for private functions or volunteer jobs.)
- Do you have a following?
- What kind of music do you play? Do you sing?
- What would you wear?
- What fee are you asking?
- When are you available?
- Do you have any references?

Questions *you* might ask:

- Whom does the clientele consist of? (businesspersons, students, etc.)
- Do you have a particular type of music in mind? (They want you to have ideas about this, too.)
- Do you allow a tip glass?
- What is the pay for overtime?

You may want to show your contract or learn whether the employer supplies one. The contract should cover payment for overtime hours.

You know, it really burns me up when I hear a mediocre musician with a good job.

Yeah, how does he get a job if he can play hardly better than me?

Performers are often judged equally on their communication skills, job-appropriate appearance and musical talent. They are also hired on their availability for the job.

86

Four performers audition. Which one has the best chance?

Chops: He shows the best technical skills, has won competitions and presents a smashing review from a local newspaper.

B+: She's a schoolteacher with lots of personality who shows versatility in her playing.

Peaches: This newcomer plays mostly pop music and is the most attractive performer.

Mel Odious: Mel is newly retired with flexible hours. Unlike the sound of many seasoned players, his music sounds fresh and rhythmic.

Who will be offered the job? It may be the person who is most AVAILABLE to play the hours needed. It may be the person who shows the most interest in the job and who follows up by contacting the potential employer. None of these four should feel competitive or intimidated, because no one knows for sure what the employer is seeking. The client will not necessarily hire the most skilled musician, but the one who can best meet his needs. All four hopefuls could be placed on the substitute list and eventually have another chance at the steady gig.

When you present yourself at an audition or interview, put on the table every valuable asset YOU have to offer. Do not take anything for granted. Even if you have mailed in a resume or tape, bring another one. While you may be confident about your sound, versatility and attire, the person before you may present several recordings he has made. On the other hand, that very person may ask for more money and turn down the employer's offer. Your group may be only average, but if the job is in a mall, and you can display madrigal costumes for a short-term holiday gig, you may well "fit the bill."

If your meeting is a simple interview, speak as positively as you would on the job itself: do not bring up anything negative about other employers, agents or previous employment situations.

Put on the table every asset you have to offer.

Approach this meeting CONFIDENT in the variety you are bringing to the whole selection process. You are guaranteed a learning experience and you are there to benefit the establishment.

Roseanne auditioned for the job of soloist in a large city church. She prepared sufficiently, but somehow took a wrong turn in her solo and made a bad impression. Yet later on, after another chance to audition, she was often asked to substitute at this church and was offered a steady job at another one.

Long range preparation for an audition

If you have a particular job in mind, find out what the job requires and begin preparing for it NOW. Example:

A large department store was under construction near Sarah's apartment. She knew the store would employ several pianists and wouldn't open for at least four months. In the meantime, she visited other branch stores to learn more about the job requirements. She learned that her repertoire should include approximately 10 different styles of music, preferably memorized, and that she would need to play with lots of smiles and eye contact. In addition, the audition would require that she submit an updated resume.

The store's recruiters did not ask for a recording, but Sarah began working on one anyway. She figured it was a good way to prepare for the audition, and they might ask for it later. After two months, she was able to play 11 very polished pieces in different styles. She produced her CD with a friend's equipment.

The morning of the audition, Sarah had a crazy idea. She bought a bag of suckers and passed them out at the audition, telling everyone she was a real sucker for a waltz. They loved it and hired her.

Four of the six pianists hired had credits and resumes more impressive than Sarah's. In fact, the store staff had mislaid Sarah's and she neglected to bring another one to the audition! Later, the store manager told her, "I hired you because I liked your spirit."

Inventing A Job

An idea for entertainment can appear any time and any place. Here are some observations a musician might make and act upon:

"That children's cable TV show band is archaic. What they need is my band. I could freshen up one of their old programs and show them what a difference my sound could make."

"The Zoo Winterfest offered some musical, acts but they needed to be more fun and less formal. How about some school kids singing country songs with guitars? It's six months away: I'll write up a proposal now."

Musician: (thinks) What can I offer my repeat customers?
Repeat customer: "Can you play at Christmastime again?"
Musician: "Sure, I can play solo or bring along a fiddle player for some stomping fiddle tunes. Would you like to hear a sample?"
Repeat: "Yes. I do like to try something different each year."

(Piano teacher sees a town banner saying Old Fashioned Days.) "I could play ragtime and have some of my students perform in costumes."

"That clown actor at the fundraiser meshed with our music so well. We could team up with him and offer the act to a party planner."

Sometimes, you may "invent" a job with hours that are more agreeable with your schedule and growing repertoire, and ask a colleague to split the hours with you.

I think I have my first real gig! It's at the Wild Oat. Five nights, six hours a night.

gag cough

That's a long time for a beginner. Can you sing and play for even three hours? It's boring to keep repeating.

I answer the phone at the stable all day. So bore me!

Couldn't you start with a weekend job?

Maybe I could find someone to split the gig with.

Nag them, maybe they'll shorten it.

A singer had an idea for a musical service in a mall setting. She made appointments with the corporate offices of two malls. The first office rejected the idea quickly. When she arrived at the second office, the secretary informed her that the manager would not be available and asked her to reschedule. After leaving, she walked around the stores ... and slowly realized that her idea wasn't suitable for this shopping area after all.

Inventive ideas are terrific, but be certain that your idea is thoroughly researched before you approach the management. Visit the place first to be sure that your idea is suitable and practical. Be able to demonstrate your new concept and prepare answers to any questions they may ask.

What's your idea?

The malls! Entertain moms while their toddlers go shopping.

Another mall opened a lavish food court. In one corner stood a grand piano with a sign on it that said, "Want to play? Contact business office from 9 - 5." They were allowing students and other amateurs to perform as volunteers, and planning to hire for the holidays.

Is there a place you can volunteer with the possibility of a paying position later? Your local mall might be very interested. Even if you offer to start playing for free, present the office with an introduction of yourself, a musical audition and your plan for the establishment.

Agents

Agents are persons who find jobs for you and take a commission, which is often 15% for a single, and 20% for an extended engagement. Large establishments have their own booking agents so that they don't have to bother with searching for entertainers. Fresh new faces like yours are often welcome. Agents can ...

- refer you for jobs you wouldn't have known about otherwise
- call you for subbing
- (in some cases) help you find auditions.

Some musicians would rather find jobs entirely on their own and avoid commission costs. If you work with an agent, be aware that the agent is liable if the musician does not show up for the engagement.

Some musicians have known agents who avoided any discussion of commission and simply asked the musician his fee, or told him what it would be. The agent then charged far beyond that amount and pocketed the difference. You can avoid this by working on a commission basis only.

If you are looking for an agent to represent you, check with friends and others for names. Pursue individuals, the phone book and business cards before investing in gig businesses on the Internet.

Provide the agent with a complete introduction of yourself. If an agent lands you a gig or an audition at an establishment, consider that place the agent's territory. Do not "go after it" on your own unless you have no intention of working with that agent in the future.

By the way, individual musicians generally do not pay other players a commission for a job referral; they simply refer one another and return the favor.

Disappointments

It hurts to have a hot job prospect fizzle. Sometimes people sound like they have some wonderful opportunity for you but nothing happens. What's worse, nothing happens after you've told everyone about it, counted on it and even worried yourself to pieces about having too much work!

Why do people make it sound like they have a job for me when they don't?

Sometimes it happens because the talker wants to impress you. Other times, the manager may be overly optimistic, thinking a musician can fit into the budget right away. Managers often need to put in much researching to find the entertainment that will meet their hours and budget and you may have simply been part of the research. Lastly, people may like you and desire to give you *something*, even if it's only a flicker of hope.

To protect yourself, don't join the motormouth brigade by telling others about "your" job. NO JOB IS A FACT UNTIL YOU ARE ACTUALLY PERFORMING AND RECEIVING A PAYCHECK.

Let's read
"Alice and the
Mad Hot-Air."

To be continued ...

January ...

Wudja do that for, I didn't do nuthin!

Q: When is a job for sure?

A: When you have your first paycheck.

Sometimes, in the midst of a disappointment, you realize that you are not being rejected; you are actually being protected!

Example:

A brass player wanted to play in the pit for a major city musical. With a Master of Music degree in hand, she scheduled an interview with the conductor. He told her she had to sight-read perfectly because his group received the music at the first rehearsal with no chance to rehearse privately. After the interview, he told her to come back after she played a few smaller shows.

It was a disappointment, but she knew her ability to concentrate and sight-read was nowhere near his expectations. Not being hired was a protection to herself and the orchestra.

Some musicians learn from disappointments; others spend their time clucking and squawking.

Mr.Cluck is still squawking because he didn't land the church choir job in his hometown, and has to travel 40 minutes to a smaller choir instead. On the other hand, the smaller church is less demanding, and the rehearsal schedule accommodates his other part-time jobs. Cluck admits, "To tell you the truth, the stress of the other job would have been fowl."

Finally, do not expect your family or friends to feel as enthusiastic about a job as you are. They have a right to their feelings and opinions, too.

Chapter Eight:
STEADY GIGS

Rules a da joint

 Help! I just started a steady job, and there's this stranger in a fedora trying to talk to me!

When you's start out at your new job, find out da rules foist. Don't barge into da kitchen for coffee—maybe dey want da waitress ta get it. Find out da procedure for breaks, food, drinks … in udda woids, learn how not to get in nobody's way!

That's good advice! Other employee dos and don'ts include:

DO use a large tip glass (generously salted ahead of time) if the management allows it.

DON'T accept any amenities from the staff (free items or privileges) that the management would not approve. These actions could result in a job loss—yours or the other employee's.

DO keep a record of your paychecks and be able to show documentation in the case of erratic or inaccurate payment.

DONT discuss personal problems on the job.

DO bring up problems to the appropriate person in order to find solutions, but DON'T indulge in gossip or aimless negative conversation.

DO be a glad-at-it-dude (that's glad-attitude): you are glad to be there, glad to play and glad to stay.

Do you take requests?

When it comes to requests, people are happy when you at least try. If someone asks for a tune that you hardly know, attempt to pick out one line of it. The person will probably say, "That's it!" He will be happy to either teach it to you or tell you more about the song.

What's really important is not your level of expertise, but your eagerness to play what people want (in addition to what YOU think is great stuff). Strengthen your repertoire by learning songs that are requested. Practice sight reading so that you can read a score or fake book with ease.

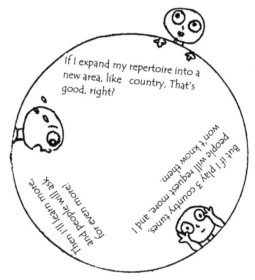

If I expand my repertoire into a new area, like country, That's good, right?

But if I play 3 country tunes, people will request more, I won't know them.

Then I'll learn more, and people will ask for even more!

Yes, the better you are, the more requests you'll get! But don't view a request as a pest that makes you appear limited. Requests are opportunities for another person to share with you and the other guests the type of music he likes. If you don't know a tune, the requester is doing you a favor by telling you about it.

When a person asks for a song that you think is silly or embarrassing, concentrate on what is attractive enough in the piece to make the person want to hear it. Is it the rhythmic drive, melody, mood or words?

Sometimes, I don't know what customers want, so I bend my head down and ignore them.

Break the ice! Ask people what they want to hear. Requests provide an opportunity for you to be friendly with your customers. If you don't know the tune, offer something similar such as a song by the same composer or a piece written in the same decade. If one person has numerous requests, keep in mind your responsibilities to the entire room, and intersperse these requests with pieces for everyone.

Classical musicians, do you hesitate to play requests because they are not arranged for your instrument? It's best, of course, to play the music as intended by the composer, but if someone wants to hear a piece, he or she will appreciate whatever you have to offer. Many books with arrangements of well-known pieces are available.

Playing more softly

Sometimes, the request is to play more softly. As a musician, you might feel humiliated by this. You wonder why you were hired in the first place. Also, it is downright difficult to play consistently with a soft volume without losing energy or tone quality. To diplomatically handle this

request:

DO keep in mind that the people actually want music. The room needs conversation AND music.

DO have someone perform a sound check. You are probably louder than you think.

DO speak cordially to the complainers and play moderately to the entire room.

Breaks

Breaks add a lot of flavor to a job. They can be useful, restful and very profitable. Customers NEED periods of quiet (ideally, not filled in with loud canned music) to appreciate the presence of a live musician. A break can last anywhere from five to 20 minutes, depending on you and your employer. Go ahead and relax on a break, but you may equally enjoy chatting with customers. People love to tell musicians about some musical relative they have, or their favorite type of music. They often have some

questions about music teachers for their kids or your availability for other gigs. Always have cards ready, because breaks can generate work!

Musicians accustomed to long stretches can easily play for one and a half hours without a break. However, audience members unaccustomed to live playing may enjoy your performance more if they see you or speak briefly with you. For this reason, short breaks with customer interaction every 45 minutes may be most effective.

Abby played background music in a lounge/restaurant and had so much fun that she often played for three hours with no breaks. Sometimes the manager would even ask her to break. (She suspected this was because no one else would listen to his tiresome jokes.) Why didn't Abby ever need a rest? The answer is that she had no musical concentration. While she played, she was indulging in every daydream that came to mind. Many gigs later, after she had become a more dedicated musician—striving to LISTEN instead of think or daydream—she needed rest times just like any other professional.

BREAKTIME
A NEW 🎲 BOARDGAME

Select a token.

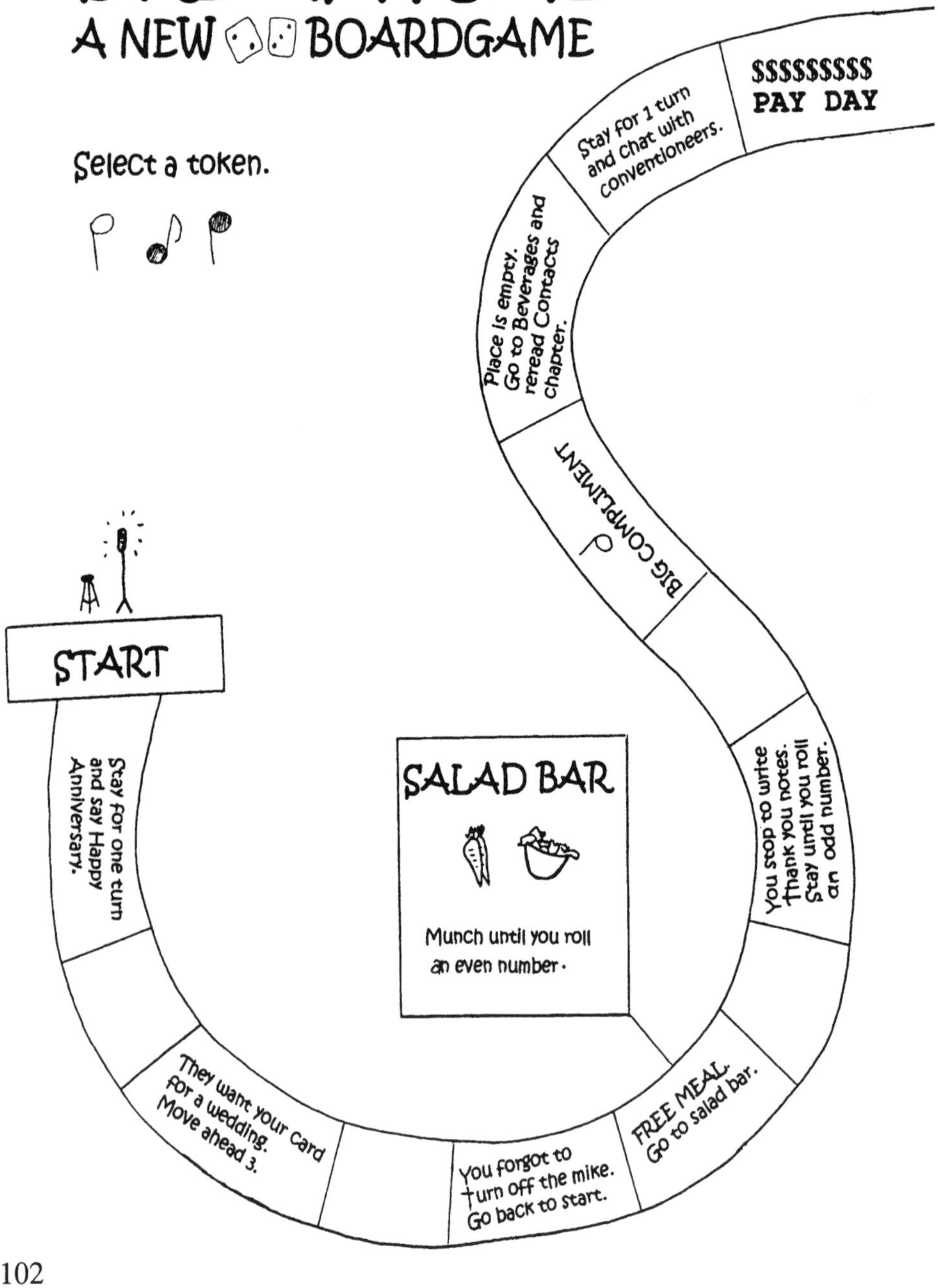

🎵 🎵 🎵

START

**$$$$$$$$$
PAY DAY**

Stay for 1 turn and chat with conventioneers.

Place is empty. Go to Beverages and reread Contacts chapter.

♪ BIG COMPLIMENT

You stop to write Thank you notes. Stay until you roll an odd number.

SALAD BAR

Munch until you roll an even number.

Stay for one turn and say Happy Anniversary.

They want your Card for a wedding. Move ahead 3.

You forgot to turn off the mike. Go back to start.

FREE MEAL. Go to salad bar.

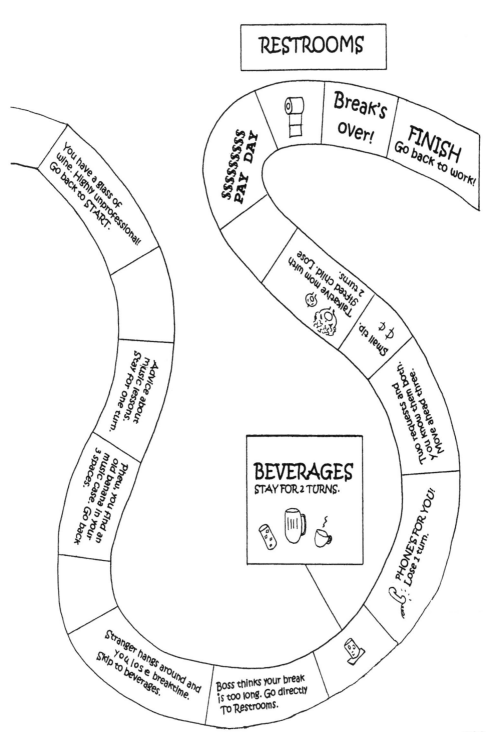

RESTROOMS

Break's over!

FINISH
Go back to work!

$$$$$$$$ PAY DAY

Talkative mom with gifted child. Lose 2 turns.

Small tip.

Two requests and both.
You know them three.
Move ahead three.

PHONE'S FOR YOU!
Lose 1 turn.

BEVERAGES
STAY FOR 2 TURNS.

You have a glass of wine. Highly unprofessional! Go back to START.

Advice about music lessons. Stay for one turn.

Phew, you find an old banana in your music case. Go back 3 spaces.

Stranger hangs around and you lose breaktime. SKIP to beverages.

Boss thinks your break is too long. Go directly to Restrooms.

Boredom on the job

Boredom need not be part of a musician's experience. You CAN enjoy playing for four hours or longer!

One reason musicians face boredom is that too often, they focus on the NAMES of the songs. Forget the names! The song becomes fresh and improved each time if you focus on a new quality you hear in it. Replace the attitude, *"I am so bored with that song!"* with goals, such as:

- I need to keep the exciting drive to the end.
- The verses need some interesting bridges.
- I have to start with the right tempo and keep it consistent.
- Get out the music and correct the errors.

Each working day, face some flaw in your playing and aim to remedy it as you play the gig. Add an improvement, such as a new piece or a corrected one. Another way to eliminate weariness or lack of concentration is to apply one general theme to the entire shift. This theme might be something you read or heard during the day. It might be one word like "motion" or "rain", or one category, such as all of the songs of a particular composer. Or, let a general concept like "love" guide your choices of repertoire. Who wouldn't enjoy that?

Boredom comes from a lack—not of customers, but of purpose or challenge. Feeling lousy about your progress leads to weariness and boredom. Regularly examine your goals, your dreams and what they have to do with this job. Can something in this gig help you work toward a higher goal?

The last hour

One more hour and the place is nearly empty. How do you get through it? Remember that every business has its lulls—discipline yourself to march through!

Pass the time:
- Play songs A – Z.
- Play a medley for every person in the room.
- Set a theme and play songs that relate to it.

Use the time:
- Throw in a very challenging piece.
- Review oldies.
- Sight read.
- Practice new, risky arrangements.

Be a Professional!
- Treat every hour alike in terms of your alertness, concentration and enjoyment.
- As a professional, your spirits are UP— with or without an audience.
- Aim for flawlessness.

Losing and Quitting

It's less upsetting to lose a job if you have been maintaining your contacts all along. Most musicians do not rely solely on one avenue of income. You need other sources, such as teaching, another part-time gig and savings, to reduce the sting of termination.

If you feel your job lacks purpose (you aren't learning anything and you aren't contributing anything), it's probably time to move on. Sometimes you can see before the management does that there is no need for your services. For example, if the bar customers are watching a football game and become annoyed by the live music, change your location fast— even if it's outside the door.

When losing or quitting:
- Be honest.
- Be brief.
- Be gracious.

Mario played the piano in an Italian restaurant for eight months. One day, the manager told him to "take the rest of the week off." He got wind from the cook that the owner wanted to give the job to a relative. Smelling the smoke, Mario told the owner that he had decided to work somewhere else. The conversation was amiable until Mario mumbled that he had been looking for a job that offered more hours, etc. The owner said firmly, "Now wait a minute. You asked for these hours. Don't act like we didn't give you what you asked for." Too bad. Mario's departure was less than graceful.

Janie never really enjoyed her weekend gig. It was dull, but at least she was performing. Suddenly, after a year and a half, she sensed that she was going to be replaced. She screamed and kicked all the way out the door. (It would have been wiser to leave graciously and obtain a good referral.) She is free now and has an opportunity for … well, anything, but her time is occupied with squawking and clucking about the dismissal.

If you lose your job, view it not as a rejection but as a protection. You are moving on to a new level of progress! You are an improved musician, and your offerings are ready to be shared in a new and better way.

Sue sensed that she had been released from her Friday happy hour gig because she had become a pest in insisting that she had not received all of her checks. In fact, she had never kept records of any checks received, so she could not back up her complaints with any dates. The management was able to prove that Sue HAD been paid accurately. She did not improve on her check recording and brought up the same problem again. The management grew tired of this and asked the agent to terminate her engagement.

Sometimes, due to poor management, payment IS slow. When you are hired, find out exactly when you are supposed to be paid and keep an accurate record of the checks you receive. If there are delays in payment, do not hesitate to speak up. If someone is being irresponsible about paying you, use the pleasant and persistent approach. Always speak about the problem **face to face with the appropriate person.**

106

Chapter Nine:
BUSINESS CARDS AND BEYOND

 Is this enough pictures of me?

When you meet a contact, you must give him something to remember you by—even if it's only a business card. If you are a soloist and perform more for a hobby than as a profession, a card may be all you need for now.

Personal contact is the best approach. People NEED smiles, enthusiastic voices and sincere interest. At this stage, you must "go after the job." A bridal couple, for example, would actively look for a musician, but a social director of a health facility needs to be reminded that Veterans Day is approaching and you have a program to share. Look for opportunities, give a smile, a greeting or tune and then a card with more information.

Most musicians experiment with different ways of promoting themselves. Every musician's presentation is different. Start with what makes *you* feel comfortable, and add on as you gain experience. Here are a few ways to represent yourself:

- Business cards: these are inexpensive and essential. A picture helps.
- Website: you can start with a free one on a social networking site.
- Professional website: more on this later.
- Brochures: websites have mostly replaced the need for brochures, but there are still persons who would rather read them than a website.
- Resume and cover letter: A resume is generally more businesslike and less creative in appearance than a brochure. It is more appropriate for acquiring steady jobs than for booking one-time gigs.

I need all
that stuff
just to start?  No, B.G., you
can start with
just a card.

Describing yourself and your services

A website is a presentation of you *and* your music. Everyone's web-site is unique and tends to be more fun and artistic than a resume. Ask yourself: Who is my target audience? What kind of work am I trying to attract? You need to show the customer who YOU are. He or she may much prefer a likeable new musician to a seasoned concert performer. Some hostesses have a soft heart for young mothers. Some hosts like reading about your hobbies or accomplishments. Include items that touch the heart, such as a thank you note from a happy customer or a picture.

Websites and brochures have the same information. Seriously con-sider your creative layout and choice of paper and font. What do you want to express? A contemporary look? A businesslike approach? Beauty and elegance? Study the websites and brochures of others. You'll get a feel for the "look" that best expresses what you have to offer. Eventually you may print a variety of cards to market yourself for different types of func-tions.

BASIC INFORMATION on a website includes:

- your name
- your instrument or ensemble instruments
- the type of music you play
- the types of occasions for which you play

- pictures or graphics to add variety
- telephone number (plus address, fax number, e-mail address or however you wish to be contacted)
- fun and meaningful extras (see below)

Extras:

- educational or performance background
- complimentary letters from customers
- news articles or reviews
- newsletters from clubs or institutions which mention your performances
- references or the statement, "references available upon request"
- hobbies and accomplishments

32nd runner-up to prom queen?

Don't haggle TOO long over the contents. Instead, consider how the brochure appears when you are performing. Is it attractive? Does it stand up, literally? Will guests spot it and walk over to read it?

Dos and Don'ts for brochure marketing:

DO address a specific person if you mail one to a host, manager, creative director or caterer.
DO show a brochure to wedding couples.
DO make your brochure as visible as possible on your gigs.
DO "follow up" or call the person ~~who~~ requested a brochure to make sure he received it.
DON'T mail out lots of "cold" brochures and expect a big response. (Hand them out in person whenever possible.)
DON'T include any statement that you can't back up with tangible proof.

Georgia! Sending out 'cold' brochures is not the best way to get work!

Georgia's ICE COLD BROCHURES

Don'tcha love the music these things play?

Advertisements: avoid expensive advertising

Musicians generally place ads in local papers and magazines. Church bulletins and university papers are helpful for wedding jobs. You can advertise for free by placing your card on store bulletin boards. If you are considering placing an ad in a particular publication, study the ads of other musicians and see what appeals to you. It helps to call the phone numbers in ads and see how they respond and what they charge.

DO repeat your ad. People respond after seeing them several times.
DON'T offer any service at which you are not proficient.
DO pick publications whose readers can afford your services.
DO call other musicians and ask if they have had successes before you spend your money.

Cover letters

You might send a cover letter with or without a brochure to a prospective employer. Years ago, a cover letter did not seem so effective; but at the time of this writing, when institutions and businesses are screaming that employees cannot write, anyone who can represent himself with a well-written cover letter has an advantage. A cover letter shows the employer your intelligence and business sense. It doesn't hurt. So, let's look at a few samples to be sure you know the basics of letter writing.

Your name
Address (include zip code)
Date

Name
Position (Director of Catering, etc)
Name of establishment
Address

Dear Ms. Devonshire (If the name is unknown, say, "Dear Sir or Madam"),

Congratulations on the opening of your new banquet facility. I am the leader of a local band called Sundown, which specializes in bluegrass music. Enclosed is a promo kit that describes our repertoire. Sundown is available to perform for receptions, parties and other events. It would be a pleasure to meet with you and audition in person. If you have any questions or would like to arrange a meeting, please feel free to contact me at 999-9999.

Best regards,
Your name

Note that the above letter begins with a positive comment. Think of something for which you can compliment or thank the person.

Dear Mr. Blake,

I truly enjoyed performing in the LaSalle Room on January 2 for the Smith reception. It was a pleasure to play in a room with such fine acoustics. I play many varieties of music and also sing, as the enclosed resume shows. Please keep my card on hand so that I may serve your establishment again.

With regards,
Your name

Note that both letters are brief. Always include a card. Many times, managers save the card and throw the rest away. Also, perfection is the rule in spelling and grammar. If you have difficulty with either one, ask someone to review your work.

♫ Gigtime Story

My grandmother was a piano player for the silent movies. She used to tell a story about an interview she had for a rare secretarial position during the Great Depression. She skillfully took dictation and typed a letter for the prospective boss, but the first thing he noticed was the salutation: "Dead sir." He said to her indignantly, "This man is very much alive. GoodBYE!" ♫

Follow up

Hello, Mr. Diddle? I sent you a music brochure last week for the Bebo duo. Do your clients ask you about reception music?

Yes, we keep a card file on musicians. Someone probably put it in there, already.

GREAT, THANKS!

It is very important to follow up a letter with a call, or a call with a letter. Early one weekday morning, a college music major telephoned a school music director and asked if the brochure she sent had been received. She enthusiastically and briefly stated her business. The director remembered this musician for years because of that call. Following up sets you apart from the piles of mail that businesses routinely receive.

I hate doing that because it makes me look desperate. I'm just another salesperson.

112

You are not a salesperson making a cold call. You have already introduced yourself through your letter.

| FOLLOW UP... Your info with a call. | Your calls with a note. |

Demo CDs

Often, musicians decide to make their first demo CD after the frustrating experience of being asked for one by an impressive contact, and having to respond, "We haven't made one." Demos take time and effort.

What should my demo CD include?

That depends on the audience you are seeking. If you want to play in a Top 40s club, then you need to record Top 40s music. It isn't necessary to play an entire piece. If your ensemble plays one style, try putting medleys together to show the listener more of your repertoire. For example, create a medley with portions of songs from the same decade. If this recording is for the purpose of booking weddings and parties, play as much variety as possible.

How many songs should I play?

Four songs played once through, or portions of up to a dozen, are appropriate amounts. Limit the number of original songs, unless that is the purpose of the recording.

How do we prepare for the recording?

If you are paying for studio time, be well-rehearsed and know exactly what you are going to play. Have all decisions concerning arrangements and repertoire worked out ahead of time. The recording will probably take more time than you had planned.

Couldn't we just record ourselves at the next party?

Don't even think about it. There would be too much noise interference.

How about if we record ourselves in a quiet living room?

It's worth a try if you have some good recording equipment.

We have a friend who offered to loan us the use of his home studio. We'll save tons of money!

You will still need a third person to operate the controls. The musician's job is demanding enough; you should not be concentrating on anything but your performance.

How would we choose a professional studio?

Ask other musicians for their opinions. Talk to the engineers of the studios they recommend and find out who records your style of music. Compare the costs of at least five studios. Listen to others recordings made in the rooms in which they intend to place you. Pianists: the instruments in recording studios range in quality. Try out the piano and hear recordings of it before you commit yourself financially.

Boomer, remember how I mailed our CD to Mr. Celebrity by certified mail?

You heard from him?

Well, not him, but his manager. Well, actually not his manager, but the office stamped it, "received".

That's all?

Boomer, WE GOT AN ANSWER!

Chapter Ten:
WEDDINGS

Helping the Couple

A wedding is such a victory; it is the couple's most exciting day so far. You have the privilege of seeing their faces up close when they say, "I do," and start crying or cracking up. It is such a treat to play a bridal processional or any wedding piece during these meaningful moments.

The first-time bride and groom have no idea how to hire people or plan a ceremony, and they really need your knowledge and enthusiasm. Usually, they're relieved to find out you already know what type of music is suitable. (You can obtain names of popular and standard wedding pieces from wedding guides and magazines.)

If you are a soloist or have a small ensemble, the couple might call you to play for the ceremony, but then have you continue during the reception until the other entertainment begins. Or yours may be the only music scheduled from beginning to end.

It makes sense to charge more if you will spend a considerable time consulting with the couple or preparing their music. The couple understands your charge if you explain, "and the fee includes arriving early, rehearsal time and helping you decide on your music."

If you mail a recording, assure the couple that it is brief one. Hiring musicians is hard work to someone who has never done it, and the bride and groom might procrastinate, regarding listening to it as a difficult chore. Do call after one week to see how they liked the music.

Before you and the bride and the groom discuss the musical details, the wedding couple should plan the ceremony with the clergy and learn any rules or customs their denominations might have regarding music. Ideally the couple can then provide you with a copy of the ceremony so everyone knows exactly where the music will fit in. The following form covers most of the details you will want to know.

MUSICIAN'S WEDDING CEREMONY INFORMATION

Date: _____

Names of bride and groom: _____

Instruments needed for ceremony: _____

Instruments needed for reception: _____

Musicians and phone numbers: _____

_____

Directions (if map is not included): _____

_____

TIMES:

Musician's arrival: _____

Prelude music: _____

Ceremony: _____

Reception: _____

SPECIFIC MUSICAL PIECES:

Preludes: _____

_____

Parent's seating: _____

Bridesmaids and children _____

Bridal Processional _____

Music during the ceremony (if program is not included): _____

_____

Recessional: _____

Post Recessional: _____

Special reception requests: _____

_____

MISCELLANEOUS:

Usher who will announce that the bridal party is ready: _____

Will a runner be unrolled before the bridal procession? _____

Number of bridesmaids: _____

Denomination of ceremony: _____

Clergy's cue to begin the recessional: _____

Length of kiss: _____ short _____ medium _____ WOW

In-home consultation

Chapter Three provides several options for letting the bridal couple hear your music. If the bride or groom received your name from a trusty referral, they may not feel it necessary to hear you at all. In other cases, the best way to book a wedding is through an in-home consultation— meaning your home, studio or practice room. It is such a pleasure to meet the couple and get to know them before their big day.

Couples go OUT to arrange flowers, tuxes and catering—why should music be any different? When they call and ask, "Is there anywhere that we could come and hear you?" you can explain, "If you stop in at one of my jobs, you might hear some requests you wouldn't want at your event. At my home I can play pieces specifically for you." If the couple comes to your home, remember that your place reflects **you** and has to be clean, tidy and professional in appearance. Some tips for the visit:

- Before the couple arrives, write a list of what you want to accomplish during the meeting.
- Limit the meeting to one half hour.
- Focus completely on your guests and their questions. If they seem serious about hiring you, ask questions from the Wedding Information Sheet.
- Show them a sample contract. They can read or even complete it while you play pieces that they can consider for their event.
- If they are interested in an ensemble, play a recording of your group.

Sometimes, the couple hiring wants to sign the contract immediately and give you a deposit. If they don't offer to sign, ask them if they would like to take the contracts home and let you know within the week so that you can secure the date. Follow up all visits with a thank you note.

Notes from A. Gigger

once I was eating dinner in my sweats and two day - old socks when the doorbell rang.

to my dismay, it was an engaged couple whose appointment I had forgotten.

the bride in her suit and briefcase gave her fiance a LOOK.

I tried, but they left. Sigh, I couldn't even finish my dinner.

Bridal fairs

A bridal fair presents an opportunity to expose your musical services to a vast number of potential customers and ideally book consultations. At this event, you rent a booth or table and display music brochures, recordings and even instruments alongside other vendors such as DJs, tux and gown shops and florists.

Jean, a mezzo-soprano, and her accompanist, Jon, shared a table at a bridal fair. Everyone seemed extremely interested in their services. Judging by the number of persons who took their cards, the duo thought they would be booked for the next five years. Then they found that the reason everyone picked up their cards was that each table was required to have a drawing or prize. Jean and Jon's prize was one hour of complimentary music valued at over $100.00. Fortunately, the winner never came forward.

Their time spent on this bridal fair totaled:

- 4 hours preparation
- 8 hours at the fair
- 2 hours contacting brides who left phone numbers on the drawing tickets.

The cost of the table and paperwork nearly equaled to one wedding reception gig. The results were a few jobs and an insight into the vast world of wedding businesses. Bridal fairs SHOULD work better than Jean's and Jon's experience, and can be worth trying. But spending a fraction of that time talking to catering directors and managers can be more profitable.

Bridal stories rated R

  B.G., you'd better stay for these true stories.

If each musician described below had been consulting a daily calendar, none of these misfortunes would have occurred.

- One Saturday afternoon while practicing, a graduate student suddenly yelped and threw her arms up in a horrible fright. She had completely forgotten about a booking to play for a wedding reception. All she could do was call the bride's father at the hotel where the dinner was taking place and apologize.

- An engaged couple hired a student duo whose resume included performing at the White House. When the couple called them to confirm two weeks before the big day, the leader, annoyed, tried to cancel because "she was preparing for her flute recital." The couple rightly insisted on holding her to the demands of the contract.

- An innocent and unsuspecting bridal couple hired two sets of musicians—one for the church, one for the hall—and NEITHER GROUP CAME.

Tales such as these illustrate how important it is for couples to hire dependable, competent musicians, instead of searching *only* for the lowest price.

You wouldn't let these horrors happen, would you? Demonstrate your dependability to each couple through a brochure or a business card designed solely for weddings. To keep their minds on music and reliability, rather than saving a few bucks, let them hear you as soon as possible.

| Have you picked a piece for your processional? | The traditional march, but maybe it's too trite. | Not at all! I could play it 1,000 times and still enjoy it. | It's always the first time for the bride, I guess. |

121

The next Mild Horror Story proves that you can't count on the couple to be responsible or reliable, either. It shows that the musician must also be firm about seeing that the contract is properly completed.

Notes from A. Gigger

i was working with a bride who was very nonchalant. i repeatedly asked her to fill in the address and directions to the church but she never did and i let it go.

on the wedding day, i entered Faith church on tenth street and waited. and waited.

i finally called her house and got a preteen bridesmaid.

like, they're all waiting for you at the church.

there were two Faith churches on the same street in the same town.

Nervousness

Why shouldn't I be nervous?

Plenty of seasoned professionals say they still get nervous before weddings. Benny, about your jitters. Maybe they happen because you have some bad habits.

- Do you daydream while you practice and give your all only at "important" occasions?

- Do you treat rehearsals casually (start late, bring unorganized music, chatter) and save professionalism for the actual gig?
- During the ceremony, do you stare at the bridal party instead of focusing on your own duties?

If a musician doesn't PRACTICE professionalism, that quality won't effortlessly appear when he performs. Give your work undivided attention during every booking, rehearsal and performance. It will make playing wedding music to a silent congregation feel more comfortable next time.

TUNEOUT'S LAMENT
"Our wedding's on the 4th of July weekend so ...

Avoid Lake Shore Drive." I said, "Okay!"
(Don't bug me, groom, it's 10 months away.)

Ten months later our trio carpooled
And that's the disaster: idle talk ruled.

Blab, blab, blab ... there's no traffic jam!
We cruised past exits and suddenly WHAM.

All cars had stopped ahead for a mile.
We weren't gonna make the march down the aisle.

Panic filled our trio's van.
Fiddler and I hopped out and RAN.

We ran from the Drive to busy downtown.
We ran in a tux and a strapless gown.

We ran in the humid midday sun.
We ran sweating buckets past everyone.

Gasping for breath I heard Fiddler say,
"This is more fun than scales all day."

We ran two miles. We ran to our doom
And tried to smile at the rabbi and groom.

A roomful was waiting, we felt like hell.
It was a sweaty Canon of Palchelbel.

But the young lovers beamed and cheered, "I do!"
The young lovers pardoned and tipped us, too.

Chapter Eleven:
ORDER IN YOUR LIFE

Using moments

Moments! I feel like I don't have ANY moments to look for new songs, make contacts, practice ...

It all sounds time-consuming, doesn't it? But most of these tasks are best accomplished by using the moments you DO have. Opportunity-filled moments can be found anywhere and anyplace.

For example, if you hear a special piece playing in another room while sitting in a restaurant with a mouthful of shrimp, be prepared to miss that one forkful and focus entirely on the song. Waiting in heavy traffic is a perfect time to compose arrangements in your head. If you happen to be dressed up, try to meet managers who would be good connections. While doing community and other volunteer work, make some new contacts.

Moments, moments, moments. But these moments don't surface by chance. They often appear when you are doing just what you are supposed to be doing. Too often, people work madly on what they WANT to do, ignoring the small, unexciting tasks they NEED to do.

Use moments in your day to meet small needs, such as answering one piece of mail or making one phone call. Make it a habit to check off one extra chore each morning (cleaning up, for example) before you leave for work or school. Habits like this will remove the clutter in your schedule and make way for more musical activity.

Planning ahead

Your tomorrow will start off on the right foot if you plan most of it today. You might develop the habit of sitting down at the end of each afternoon and jotting down what you need to accomplish in the following day. Some people use Mondays to set a few goals for the week ahead. Certain goals that they don't touch become top priorities for the following week.

Although Andre, a cellist, graduated from high school eight years ago, he still remembers the English teacher who regularly gave his class a daily quiz of five questions. To save paper, the students would fold one piece in quarters and use one quarter for each day's test. Reviewing the entire sheet of quiz grades on Fridays was a good way for the students to

126

judge their progress. Folding an 8 1/2" x 11" piece of paper in quarters became a good weekly organizer for Andre, and he still uses this tool. On the first square, he writes general goals for the week. Each day has one square. Toward the end of the day, he writes down what needs to be accomplished the next day. He keeps this quartered sheet with his calendar.

Part of today's job is preparing for the next day. Near the day's end, spend a few minutes making a list for tomorrow on your own quartered sheet. *THEN LOOK AT TODAY AND RECOGNIZE THE GOOD THINGS THAT HAPPENED.* It would be unbalanced to continually plan your next days without also reflecting back on all of the big and small accomplishments of the current day.

The Plan Pan

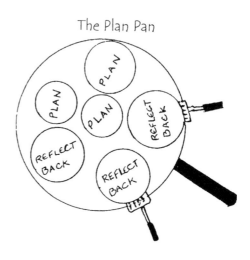

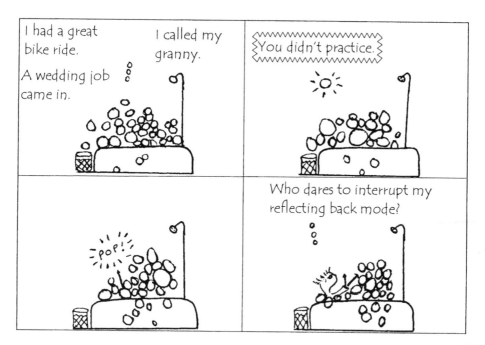

Preparing for the holidays

Oh boy, look what's coming up in December. The following calendar shows the gig dates of a part-time musician's holiday month. It includes not only extra jobs, but extra rehearsals for some of these as well. How will the musician prepare for this avalanche of work?

DECEMBER

SUNDAY	MONDAY	TUESDAY	WEDNESDAY	THURSDAY	FRIDAY	SATURDAY
	1	2	3	4 *classical gig*	5	6 *background music*
7	8	9 *Hanukkah party*	10	11	12	13 *Christmas tunes*
14 *ensemble playing*	15	16	17	18 *ensemble gig*	19	20
21	22 *office party*	23	24 *church service*	♩ 25 *church service*	26	27
28	29	30	31 *New Year's party*			

It's November 1 and I've already started! I sight-read two pieces each day to prepare for December 4th and the services. By then, I'll either have memorized the pieces or feel very comfortable reading on the job. Ensemble rehearsals will be on November 16 and 23. For now, all I need to do is listen to holiday tunes and get in the mood!

If you do things in an orderly way, you generally won't need to push or rush. Besides the weekly quartered sheet, a few other basic tools (or expenses) will help you be a calm, orderly professional:

- Always have your CALENDAR with you.
- Keep a NOTEBOOK updated with your practicing goals and growing repertoire.
- Save the BUSINESS CARDS of your contacts and fellow musicians (preferably in an alphabetized container).
- Answer PHONE and other messages promptly.
- Maintain FILES (you can start with a cardboard box) of articles, notes and programs that will help you in the future.
- Store contracts in two files or FOLDERS for contracts, labeled "contracts, confirmed" and "contracts, unconfirmed." Keep these files near your phone.

I have to get all this stuff today?

No, B.G. Start working and add the professionalism as you can.

- STATIONERY: You need appropriate paper for thank you notes, introductory letters, occasional bills and short notes. Plain white 5" x 7" notepad paper is adequate. Always include a personal note or comment when you send a CD or brochure. For brides, you could include a wedding card. Splurge on luxurious writing paper if you can; it acknowledges the importance of the event.

Completing tasks

ORDER requires a calm and careful beginning, middle and end. When preparing for gigs, check every detail the day or days before. This includes confirming the job with the host and having your music, directions, equipment and attire ready. Thorough preparation like this helps you be the relaxed, confident person the job demands. After you perform, don't consider the job finished until you unpack, make appropriate contacts (this actually could be done on a break instead of later at home) and file the contract.

Ψ THE COMPLETE GIG ☿

Arriving at work promptly

Why is it so hard for some people to be on time? What are the obstacles that keep them from arriving on time? Being prompt takes accurate PLANNING. Late people falsely estimate how long it takes to get ready and arrive when they are expected .

Musician #1: I have no problem being on time for a steady gig because I follow a routine. It's when the job is a one- timer that I tend to rush, get lost and drive with my stomach in knots because there's not one minute to spare. I walk into the job smiling but completely frazzled.

If you arrive in a frantic state of mind, you can be sure that feelings such as tension, inhibition and fear have tagged along, too. It takes extra effort, but you must carefully calculate how long your commute will take, allowing for traffic, bad weather, etc. Don't take chances with directions: bring a map along. Plan to arrive early with extra work to do, such as notes to write or calls to make.

But is that fair? They are not paying me for those extra minutes.

In this case, you are self-employed and paying yourself by using the time as you would at home.

Musician #2: I consistently come to my steady gig five minutes late and I know why—I am mad at them for not paying me enough.

Payment is the heart of the problem. You sure won't get a raise by being late. Being prompt is part of being a professional and has nothing to do with how much you are earning. Reread the chapter on payment.

By the way, if you arrive five minutes late every day, your first set must feel like chaos! Some musicians make it a habit to arrive 20 minutes early—especially for ensemble gigs. This shows the leader that they are dependable and puts the host of the event at ease.

Chapter Twelve:
ACCOMPANYING

The demand for classical accompanists

If you are either a classically trained keyboardist or one who plays from music, rather than by ear, accompanying is an opportunity you should consider. The demand for student and adult accompanists is great, particularly in the spring when recitals, school shows and competitions abound. Accompanying lets you join in the excitement of participating without feeling the pressure of being a soloist. It also offers the chance to meet other musicians and provide a tremendous service.

Here's a warning: once you start accompanying, you can expect the requests to multiply year after year, especially if you keep the names of teachers and schools in your "tickler file" and periodically remind them that you are available. Musicians with keyboard/vocal degrees have been known to work their way into faculty positions by starting out as music department secretaries, gradually adding on accompanying jobs for faculty and student recitals. Larger universities sometimes employ full-time accompanists. What a gig!

Who needs accompanists?

Theatres
- comedy acts
- professional musicals

- amusement parks that feature live shows
- community groups
- children's theatre

Voice teachers
- student recitals
- rehearsals
- competitions

Dance studios
- recitals
- rehearsals

Churches
- services
- choir rehearsals

Schools
- grade school/high school musicals
- special holiday events
- after-school music groups
- voice/band/orchestra competitions

These people and places are glad to learn of musicians—capable students included—who can substitute as accompanists. Schools and private teachers, in particular, need accompanists for spring activities, particularly. In churches, a few subbing jobs could lead to a steady position. A lack of newly degreed organists has created a demand for musicians to fill in for retiring organists. Many churches are willing to either buy a piano and hire a pianist, or find a keyboardist willing to train to play the organ. Church accompanying is steady, reliable work. The discipline it entails keeps a musician's technique and accompanying skills in prime condition for other musical opportunities.

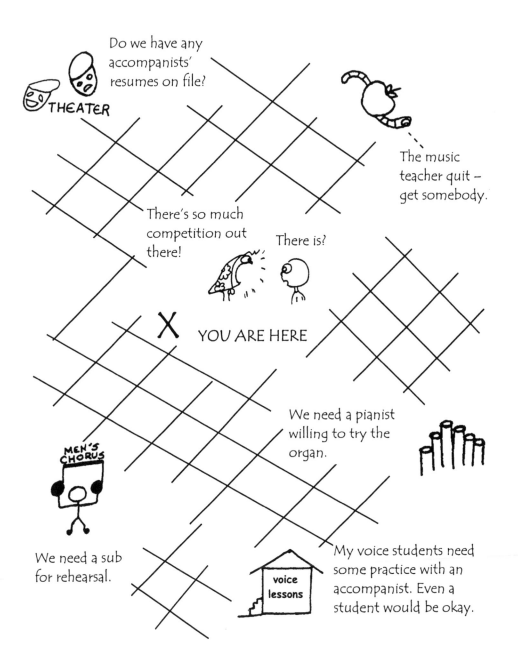

THEATER

Do we have any accompanists' resumes on file?

The music teacher quit – get somebody.

There's so much competition out there!

There is?

X YOU ARE HERE

We need a pianist willing to try the organ.

MEN'S CHORUS

We need a sub for rehearsal.

voice lessons

My voice students need some practice with an accompanist. Even a student would be okay.

135

Musical productions

If you do not have time to attend many rehearsals, but are willing to accompany the actual performance, you can contribute by recording the rehearsal music. Some schools and community theaters have a budget for professionally recording the music and also using it for the performance. Example:

Gordon was offered a spring accompanying position at a children's theater. It was impossible to accept—the job involved a 45-minute commute, and a commitment of three to four days per week. Since his schedule was packed, Gordon declined.

But one Sunday morning, he started thinking about the theater and felt bad. The job was no prize, but he still really wanted to help the staff. Suddenly, it occurred to him: "Why don't I offer to record the music; at least they'll have something until they get a pianist." He immediately rang up the director, who was more than happy to be called on a Sunday morning if the call could lead to finding an accompanist.

Gordon ended up making a professional recording backed by a drummer, that was used as the theatre's performance music. He was paid well for his work and was invited back for the next show. It turned out to be a great learning opportunity—while Gordon was already an experienced accompanist, the mental and physical demands of studio recording pushed him even further and opened the door to more studio work.

♪ Gigtime Story

A high school in a high-crime area needed an accompanist for a spring competition. When I arrived at the school to rehearse, a normal day was in progress with police cars on patrol and security guards positioned up and down the halls. I tried to walk into the washroom marked "Girls", but one guard insisted I use the nicer one, the teacher's restroom. This one had cracked and peeling walls, a broken clock and a toilet and pipes repaired with duct tape. Stunned, I cut my fee considerably.

Anyway, the soloists rehearsed fairly well, considering that none of them took private lessons and they had prepared completely on their own. Shell was particularly memorable. Very husky and very sweet, he played a slow, soulful piece on his clarinet.

Shell arrived for the competition all dressed up in an ill-fitting dark green suit and fuzzy black earmuffs. This seemed strange, but I was in foreign territory. I figured the earmuffs were some kind of headphones. Shell didn't let on that he was extremely nervous.

We greeted the judge and started tuning up. The judge said, "Hey, is it cold in here?" "No, not at all," we answered. "Then why do you have your earmuffs on?" the judge asked Shell.

Shell turned to me and demanded incredulously, "WHY DIDN'T YOU TELL ME I HAD MY EARMUFFS ON?"

Oh, that was my responsibility. After all, I was the accompanist. He removed them and played just fine. ♪

Gigs on vacation

Next time you travel, prepare to make a few contacts. Wouldn't it be nice to **perform** at the locale you're enjoying? If you can fulfill a demand for a good accompanist, opportunities exist to do just that.

How can I find opportunities like that?

Start with these ideas:
• Work for singers who take their acts to resorts.
• Contact theatres in locations where you would like to visit.
• Contact touring musicals or shows.
• Contact cruise ships, as well as agents who handle cruise ships.

Skills

Accompanying usually demands the skills of being musically supportive, leadership and sight reading. Let's examine each of these traits.

Support

As an observer, have you ever cringed through a performance because the accompanist did not give the soloist enough bass? The accompanist's job is to provide support. Both classical and non-classical accompanists must discern the needs of the soloist or singing group.

If the soloist is weak, he needs you to guide him along by playing the melody. If the person is a strong performer, playing the melody actually is a hindrance (unless the score demands it). All singers need plenty of supportive BASS. Finally, soloists and choruses depend on the introduction to know the tempo and beat of the song; there is no reason to slow down during the introduction, unless the song is a ballad.

Support, *v.*
1. to uphold by aid or encouragement.
2. to keep from falling or sinking.
3. to accompany.

Georgia's comments on support:

"Musician who buys strapless gown worries not about cost but about upkeep."

Leadership

As the accompanist, you sometimes are the leader of the group. If this is your role, arrive at the rehearsal completely organized with goals to be accomplished within a set time frame. Charging by the hour will help keep an adult group from spending too much of your time socializing or discussing. The more professional you act, the more efficiently work will be accomplished. Remember, professionalism includes a happy attitude and generous PRAISE and ACKNOWLEDGEMENT for improvements and work well done.

Sight reading

Hats off to any musician who is able to sight-read for hours at a time: he or she has either years of experience or nerves of steel. If you must sight-read accompaniments (at musical play auditions, for example) proceed this way:

1. Have the actors perform their monologue first, giving you time to study their music.
2. Look at the key signature and meter.
3. Scan the piece for accidentals, changes of key or other "tough spots."
4. Discuss the tempo and repeats with the performer ahead of time.

Fudging the notes

Yuko took an accompanying course for a music degree requirement. She learned how to "fudge," or omit unnecessary notes in order to better sight-read. While this was definitely a helpful skill, Yuko used it regularly in accompanying jobs afterwards, instead of practicing efficiently in order to learn all of the notes. Then, she was hired by a theater company to record a musical score, note for note. Her work was inaccurate, and several expensive recording hours were wasted because she was so unaccustomed to playing all of the notes. Like the food, fudging can be a dangerous habit!

Accompanying shows

Only a good accompanist knows how much a performance depends on the accompaniment. If you miss a beat or an essential part of the accompaniment, the amateur singer usually falters without knowing why. Attention, accompanists: you can help most ensemble problems by **CTA**: (Checking The Accompaniment) and correcting or improving your own part.

Problem: Soloists are insecure at the beginning of the song.
CTA: Do they know the full introduction, with the proper rhythm?

Problem: The chorus is not singing in the tempo you are playing.
CTA: More bass is needed.

Problem: The piece needs to be more of a show-stopper.
CTA: Are you playing all of the notes? If you are the arranger, is the ending appropriate to the song, in terms of length and character?

Problem: The singer is ... well, pretty bad.
CTA: Does the music need to be transposed?

Dos and Don'ts for accompanying musicals:

DO pay 100% attention to your cues from the very first rehearsal.
DO polish your solo parts from the very beginning.
DO be willing to transpose if it truly will aid the singer.
DON'T slow down during the introduction, thinking it will help the singer enter.
DON'T drop out the bass because you have a page turn.
DON'T fudge it—learn the notes, unless your own arrangement is better

and supports the singer equally well.

Improvising

Accompanying often requires slipping in tidbits of music here and there, such as during scene changes and other "empty" spaces of a show. In these instances, improvising means filling up silent moments with something you have already played. To avoid lags in the program, be alert to moments that need filler.

Being on cue

What if every actor and musician always was perfectly on cue? Wouldn't that save an enormous amount of rehearsal time? Accompanying shows requires much waiting for your cue. Being alert and timely, at rehearsals as well as performances, is just as important for accompanists as it is for the actors onstage.

In rehearsal, have amateurs SPEAK THEIR CUE LINES before you play the introduction of their song. You both need to feel comfortable with this transition from script to song.

Experienced singers will expect you to follow **them**, and take slight musical pauses when they breathe. Some vocalists ask the accompanist to literally take breaths when they do. Singers also need accompanists to be flexible—to change tempos and styles when appropriate.

Knots in your stomach

Sometimes a challenging job makes you feel like a wreck, and you want to quit. Maybe another person even advises it. Be careful—quitting will only postpone problems. Most likely, you need to hang in there and march through your nervousness and inexperience and on to victory!

142

Adding sing-alongs to your gigs

A sing-along is a magic moment. Every sing-along group is one of a kind. This activity adds a liveliness and a unity to the gathering that entertains even those who didn't join in.

Singing used to be a national pastime. The older the crowd, the more likely you will find enthusiastic singers. Younger generations still want to sing, but often they are bashful—partly because music is given so little priority in education today. But their ability to sing is still there, however, and you must encourage it!

Sing-alongs give you a competitive edge in your fees: you can charge slightly less for three hours, figuring that you will easily make it up, and more, in overtime pay. The host will be happy to pay overtime if guests are bellowing and having a great time.

You expect me to
have a sing-along?

You can! If you play an instrument that doesn't lend itself to leading a group, try the autoharp as a second instrument. It's simple to play and works great for children's parties.

When you and the host are planning the event, suggest a sing-along. The more support you have from the host at the actual event, the more likely the guests will respond. At the party, stay on the lookout for persons who particularly respond to the music or like to sing. On your break, walk around the room and let people know you brought song sheets. Start the singing by setting an example. Don't worry ... your job is not to impress anyone as a soloist (although that ability has its place at a party too), but to bring out the best in those around you. If only one or two people respond, don't give up; it's likely to grow. Sometimes, even the most unlikely people really do want to take part.

I remember leading a sing-along at which a beautiful woman who looked like a glamorous actress stood awkwardly nearby. Although she wanted to join in, she said, "But I can't sing," and left. It was really sad! I wished I could have given her more encouragement.

Every sing-along is different. Since there might be slightly awkward moments when nobody can think of what to sing next, keep playing quiet backup music. If someone asks for a song you don't know, let him croon away and try to back him up with basic I, IV and V chords. The more you attempt this improvising, the easier it will become. Go with the spontaneous flow of the party, focusing on how to help the event.

Suggestions for sing-alongs

1. Use song sheets. This puts you in control and eliminates many requests you may not know.
2. To avoid long pauses, plan the next song before the current one ends. Encourage the guests to call out their favorites.
3. Vary the routine—play some tunes once and some twice, occasionally adding your own solo part in the middle.
4. Sing with the group. A mediocre voice is fine—it encourages the timid ones.
5. For average singers, keyboardists should play with a strong, straightforward melody and a firm beat. The singers need either a strong lead voice or a loud melody to lead them. Listen to the voices.
6. If you can, repeat the best songs in a higher key—milk the momentum.
7. If children are present, start with songs *they* can sing. They will lure the adults into the sing-along.

Making your own song sheets

- Appeal to all ages. Some booklets categorize the songs (i.e., one page of children's, one patriotic page, pop, etc.).
- Include songs that YOU know and like.
- Use large print, and number each song.
- Give nursing homes and other institutions one copy and have them provide the rest if possible.

The sing-along that wasn't

Chris thought the party would feature a holiday sing-along, but there was not much support from the hosts and she couldn't get it going. The gig was a letdown—nothing but ear-splitting talking for three hours.

She decided that her function was simply to provide technically excellent music with much variety. She made use of the time by trying some demanding music, knowing the din would cover up any blotches.

At the end, the hosts were very complimentary and tipped generously, which doesn't necessarily happen even at a successful party. Oh well, it pays the bills!

THE SING-ALONG

They're all singing; it's going great!	What's the next song?	Got it, whew.
This is fantastic; they're deafening!	I can't think of what to play after this.	Whew! There it is.
Gee, the next song is ...	Always there.	Every time!

146

Chapter Thirteen:
WHAT ABOUT TEACHING ?

Thinking about it

These two careers can work together tremendously: teaching makes you a better performer, while performing makes you a more inspiring teacher. Because gigs often do not provide a steady source of income, many musicians rely on private or classroom teaching for a regular paycheck.

You don't always need a degree in music education to teach. Some private schools and preschools are willing to hire musicians with different types of degrees or who still are students themselves. In many states, sufficient teaching experience can help you earn a Substitute Teachers Certificate qualifying you to sub in public schools, which offer higher pay. Having tried the work part-time, you may wish to pursue a degree enabling you to work full-time.

The other route to a teaching position is to head straight for a music education degree. If this degree has always been your goal, you are being very practical; studying music education now will help you avoid future schooling time and tuition costs later on. If you want to do something with music but aren't sure what, an Ed degree is a wise and practical choice. It will help you in whatever musical direction you take.

Are you a parent concerned about the cost of preschool or private school? Some institutions (especially preschools and day care centers)

are happy to arrange a barter of your teaching time in exchange for free or reduced tuition for your child.

I play keyboards and I can't sing at all. Must you be able to sing to teach in a classroom?

Not necessarily. You could be an outstanding teacher without a performer's vocal ability. However, look at how singing is defined:

sing, *v.*
1. to produce musical sounds or notes with the voice.
2. to be exultant; to rejoice.
3. to celebrate.

Hey, my voice can sound like that!

148

Notes from A. Gigger

it all started in high school. i
played in the band, but never
sang in the chorus or shows.

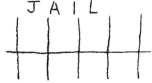

by the time i was in college, i
wouldn't sing for anybody! but
singing and playing go together,
so i had to learn.

sing + play = job

i really tried! i took years of voice
lessons, but my heart wasn't in it.

(ACTUAL WORDS OF TEACHER)

"I'm sicka dis horse____"

i gave up. my voice was behind bars.

then, a private school asked me to
teach general music.

suddenly, i had to sing, four hours
at a stretch! and to my surprise, i
loved teaching the kids.

i found my niche. teaching
school improved my voice
enough to sing when i needed
to on the job!

Brendan the music teacher/performer

Brendan teaches middle school ensemble music Monday through Friday, then gigs on the weekend. He is working too hard!

I am stressed out trying to keep up with customer requests, school music, private students' music ... plus the arranging I really want to do!

Brendan, you can do some recycling and unify all these tasks. Take a favorite song and spread it all over—not only to save yourself time, but because everyone deserves to hear it! One simple song can be used and shared several different ways. Here's an example:

1. A private student brings Brendan a tape of a pop tune. He makes notating the melody part of her ear-training study.
2. Brendan learns the tune, and it becomes an often-played, current song for his weekend gig.
3. He arranges the piece for his combo, which performs it at a wedding.
4. He teaches the song in three-part harmony to his school chorus.

Brendan, are you bored with the song?

No. It's being heard in so many ways, and everybody likes it.

Performing and teaching work together

They sure complement one another!

- Your students keep you up-to-date on the latest tunes and the type of music that interests young people.
- Your performance skills stay sharp when your lesson plans include playing.
- Clapping out rhythms with students improves your own sight reading.

150

- Becoming comfortable with children will help you provide better services on many gigs.
- You can test new musical ideas in the classroom.
- Teaching alerts you to every person in the room.
- Teaching expands your knowledge of music and makes you a more balanced musician.

A sample of classroom teaching

Mia was a young mother who held three part-time music jobs and taught one day a week in a suburban school. This particular school housed all of the kindergarten children of that school district. The diversity in this suburb was so immense, that one year there were 28 languages spoken at the school. Mia's position required teaching general music to ten classes in a day. Two of the classes included children with mental disabilities and one of the classes was ESL (English as a Second Language.)

Mia was thrilled with her public school income after five years of teaching in private schools. (The income was more than double.) The work was easy—kindergarten students don't generally have music homework or tests—and Mia was very experienced in maintaining an orderly, disciplined classroom of children this age. If anything was a challenge, it was in handling the boredom of teaching the same material to ten classes in a row. Sometimes, at the end of the day, she was eency spidered out!

151

Mia was given much freedom in choosing her lesson plan material (as many music teachers are) and she kept the classes lively and interesting with creative movement and dancing.

One day, the children performed creative movements to a taped piece which contrasted music from Greece, China, India and Japan. Mia played this cultural piece two or three times for each class, meaning that she listened to it more than 25 times. As soon as Mia arrived home, however, she played the same tape for her own kids! She said to her husband, "What's the matter with me? I heard a piece 25 times today and I'm not tired of it!" He smiled and replied, "YOU'RE A MUSIC TEACHER."

Private teaching

Most musicians have taught privately at one time or another. It's natural to share what you know, right? Private teaching can be satisfying and successful if it is treated like a business (with the strictest of tuition and cancellation policies) AND you have a genuine desire to teach.

I'm not a degreed musician. Am I qualified to teach privately?

Independent teaching is one type of teaching that does not require any degree. It is surprising, the number of people who are willing to start lessons with a teacher without ever asking about the teacher's degrees or other credentials. If people hear you play well and you seem friendly and amiable, it often leads to the question, "Do you teach?"

I could teach beginners, in fact, a number of parents have asked me about it.

Be clear about what you are able to teach at present. What do you know that could set you apart from other local teachers? Perhaps you have a strong blues background, or a gift for arranging.

How can I find students?

Many ideas in the Contacts chapter will help. Place brochures or cards wherever parents and children , starting with grade school bulletin boards (with the school's permission). The best way is through referrals. Send a resume and cover letter to all of the music teachers in your area, explaining that you are a new teacher and would appreciate their referrals if they have waiting lists. Add teaching to your business card and be ready for the inevitable question on your gigs, "Do you teach?" As part of your teaching business, you will always be putting some time and energy into finding new students.

What would I charge?

Ask the teachers in your area what they charge. You can charge more if you are willing to teach in people's homes.

How can I combine individual and group lessons?

Some teachers combine their students once every six weeks. This lesson serves as a performance goal and is a good time for theory games, note drills and ensemble playing.

I'm already teaching eight students but cancellations are a problem. Parents cancel lessons in lieu of sporting events, plays and birthday parties.

Some teachers use a tuition plan which includes payment on a quarterly basis (payment being due on the first week of a three month period).

All make-ups are saved for a particular week—perhaps group lesson week or when school is out. Some teachers only allow make-ups with a 24 hour notice. Along with your tuition information, state your studio rules and keep them.

♪ Gigtime Story
As a child, I took lessons in a mansion that had been converted into a convent on acres of spacious grounds. Ancient (or so we thought) nuns

would greet children at the heavy fortress-like door and usher them into a lush parlor with a giant mahogany staircase, velvet draperies and a terrifying statue of an angel in armor killing a devil with curly hair and horns.

My teacher came from a wealthy Irish family. She happily passed up most luxuries and the opportunity to develop her own performance talents to lead a selfless life devoted to teaching little ones. Over and over again she said, "Music makes a happy home." ♫

HOME SWEET HOME

Chapter Fourteen:
YOU AND THE PEOPLE

Customers say things such as:

- What was the name of the song you played about 45 minutes ago?
- I took lessons when I was 10 and …
- That was my dad's favorite song.
- It might seem like no one is listening but we're really enjoying your music.

Hooray for customers! They create the evening, don't they? A customer is a walking suggestion of what to play next. Sometimes a customer gives you an earful of confidences and stories about themselves. People want to share their feelings about music or perhaps a memory of how they grew up with it. Customers make jobbing a very social activity.

Shyness and self-consciousness

Yup, they're the last things you need on a gig. In any career, shyness and self-consciousness need to be overcome. Your shyness makes your customers think you don't appreciate them. If shyness causes you to be tongue-tied or aloof, it can even deeply offend a customer.

Sometimes, I just clam up. I feel so uncomfortable, just when I should be happy and relaxed.

Perhaps a few professional habits could improve your comfort level.

Like what?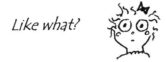

1. **Being on time:** plan to arrive early. Bring some extra work to do.
2. **Wearing appropriate attire:** find out ahead of time exactly what the occasion will be and how you should dress.
3. **Focusing on your musical purpose (rather than yourself):** this especially applies to feeling like a misfit on breaks. As you walk through the room, keep in mind your purpose for being there. Remind yourself that your music is enriching the event.
4. **Being musically prepared:** thoughtfully assemble your music and equipment the day before.
5. **Thinking about customers in a positive way:** observe your audience only for the purpose of serving them.

He's too old for her.

I wonder if that chest is real.

B.G., cut the kid stuff!

cling clang rattle

6. **Developing musical confidence:** gain experience by performing more often. Even charity jobs will give you what you need most—experience. You may feel nervous and awkward because you are overly impressed with the employer or audience. The solution to this discomfort is to treat everyone the same: professionally provide the flawless service that is needed and keep your mind on only your duties.
7. **Feeling comfortable with silent listeners:** often, you have to break the ice and ask people outright what kind of music they want to hear. This effort at friendliness will loosen everyone up.

156

To help others overcome shyness and self-consciousness, Georgia is marketing a luxurious portable commode.

157

Well, I still get sweaty when people are listening.

Seasoned players sometimes do, too. But imagine this: you are the driver of an excursion boat. Everyone piles in and you're off for an adventurous ride. You hear people laugh and shriek when a wave splashes onto the deck. Why are all these people on the boat? They are there to feel the magical movement of the water. They aren't thinking about the driver! In both practicing and performing, strive to keep thoughts about yourself OUT and completely submit to enjoying and improving the music.

Unmannerly customers

A bothersome customer SHOULD be the exception, even a rarity. But since it happens occasionally, let's look at the problem.

As musicians, we're supposed to serve others.

And allowing anyone to be a pain is not doing him a service.

Let's say your function is to supply background music, and a customer oddly hangs around for a long period of time or makes continual comments. In this case, you can take a cue from school teachers. A good teacher is positive that every student has something worthwhile to contribute. Sometimes, steps must be taken to elicit good behavior from a student and keep the classroom in control. For example, if a student is loitering around the classroom, the teacher has the student sit down.

In the same vein, a musician cannot perform at his best when a customer acts inappropriately. Your solution is to channel that behavior into an appropriate activity. Ask the person to have a seat. Say nicely that you cannot perform and hear talking at the same time. Offer a pen and ask him or her to write down his numerous requests—ones that would really work on your instrument. Keep any conversation focused on music.

Now, check your own response. Your aim is to have so much confidence in the message of your music that another's actions cannot fluster you. If somone CAN throw you off, this experience is a good music lesson. The annoying actions of this person are just bringing to light an area in which you need to improve.

If you have a basic respect for and appreciation of the customer, you will be in control of situations where manners are in short supply. If you feel upset and resentful, you are powerless to improve the situation.

Intoxication

If you are having problems with people who are intoxicated, tell the manager. These offenders are probably bothering other staff and customers, too. If you constantly deal with customers who are offensive because of the effects of alcohol, search for other musical opportunities. See "Contacts", "Accompanying" and other chapters of this book for ideas.

Mel was a piano bar performer. At first, she had one focus; to support herself through music, no matter what the job was. Slowly, it dawned on her that the lounge's purpose in hiring her was to have people order more drinks (and then drive home). This bothered her, so after her contract ended, she concentrated on booking parties and receptions. She also accepted a part-time teaching position. It has been 15 years since she played in a bar and she leads a versatile life as a musician.

That one guy was obnoxious. + +	He yelled across the room for me to liven it up. (◎ ◎)	But he made me see what the party needed. ◉ ◉
Then he started singing and made the party a lot of fun. ◎ ◎	 ◔ ◔	Swell guy. ( ) ◡

Prevention of sexual harassment

Tina played background music in a quiet room on Friday nights. She distinctly remembers two instances of customers standing next to her for over an hour—staring, giving advice and occasionally making suggestive comments. In both cases she realized afterwards that although the **other persons were completely out of line**, the situations could have been prevented if her attire and speech had been completely professional. (It would have been acceptable to ask to the customers to have a seat, also.) She needed to be cordial, but focused on music only.

Maybe she was helping the customer by pretending to listen and being nice.

It is not "nice" to allow others to act inappropriately. To avoid un-
wanted conversation or conduct, Tina learned to check herself first and
ask, "Is there ANYTHING in my appearance, eye contact or mental attitude that is less than professional?" Professionalism eliminates, (or at
least reduces) these types of situations. Do not allow customers to draw
you into more than brief conversation while you are working.

Senior centers

Performing for seniors groups is a fine way to gain experience and
also reach out to the community. Because they grew up with it and are
trained to appreciate it, persons of this generation are usually very respon-
sive to live music.

Maybe so, but sometimes there are problems from the first call.

Like what?

Sometimes they talk at length with details I don't need.

Pay close attention—there may be a problem here to prevent. Discuss
ahead of time what the needs and desires of the group are.

Seniors come early and watch us set up and offer advice.

Relax—they just enjoy watching, that's all. Greet the group and then
concentrate as you would on any job. At least the gig will start on time.

There are volume complaints.

Dos and Don'ts for seniors:

DO plan ahead of time for the tables to be placed at a comfortable distance
from the music.
DO discuss the volume with the contact person and be sure anyone with a
hearing aid is seated far away. (Hearing aids often produce a ringing
sound for the wearer.)

161

DON'T underestimate the happiness you are bringing to people through your individual attention, kindness, smiles and willingness to "give a listening ear" on breaks or afterward.

DO make friends with guests at the tables nearest you before you start playing. They will be more likely to support you rather than complain about the sound level.

DO turn down the volume if requested to do so.

Children

Children on a gig are not dull. They …

Crave Christmas songs all year round.
Handle your instrument, cards and personal space with sticky fingers.

Interrupt the song they requested with another … and another.
Liven up parties with singing and dancing.
Drag their parents and grandparents over, making the event really start!
Respond to the music with wide, appreciative eyes.
Enjoy your music much more than the main course.
Need to hear their requests played SIMPLY.

 I was trying to perform, and these youngsters were all over me, interrupting and touching.

Many gigs include no personal contact with children. However, if you do perform around families, it helps to know a few things about kids. Often, they take their cue from you. If you smile, they will smile back. If you talk, they may think it is okay to have a conversation with you while you are trying to perform. They often need to be gently taught that they shouldn't touch your instrument without permission. Children will do what you ask of them as long as they can sense that you genuinely appreciate and enjoy them.

If the problem is that they keep interrupting you with requests, tell them that they need to wait until the current song is over to ask for another one. If they touch your instrument or bang on it, hold your hands at your sides and say, "Can you keep your hands like this?" Channel inappropriate behavior into something better. If the child is very young you might say; "This is a dancing song. Would you show me how you can spin around (or tap your feet, etc.)?" Engage their participation in clapping, snapping or singing. Remember—this is a special experience for them, and it may be their first experience with a musician.

Children's parties

Maybe your niche is children's parties. If you are a parent, teacher, camp counselor or day-care provider, you already know how to handle a group, as well as the games and songs children enjoy. If your function is to make music WITH the kids (as opposed to putting on a concert), you need a lesson plan similar to one that a teacher uses. For a half-hour program, prepare a plan of five or six activities. Be sure to highlight the honoree with a special song and allow that child to have the first turn. Try the following suggestions for parties with children ages seven and under:

- Have a sing-along of songs the children already know (plan ahead of time with a parent).
- Bring a collection of rhythm instruments to share.
- Teach one or two new songs they can easily sing and perhaps play along or clap to.
- Show a picture book and play a recorded piece.
- Play musical games with live accompaniment. "Musical chairs" is a favorite. You can use placemats instead of chairs.
- Teach simple dance steps.

Ideas for ages eight and above:
- Stage a talent show (plan with parent ahead of time).
- Have a sing-along with song sheets.
- Teach simple dance steps.
- Have a dance contest.
- Play musical bingo or "Name That Tune." (You can find more musical games at the library or a music store.)

Chapter Fifteen:
TUNES AND EARS

Adding to your repertoire

What's in your repertoire?

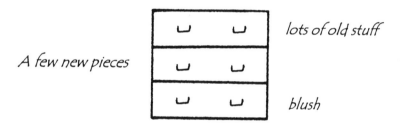

A few new pieces

lots of old stuff

blush

Repertoire IS like a top drawer: it needs to be inspected once in a while.

So you have a growing repertoire. Naturally, it's based on music to which you are attracted. But your repertoire could expand even more by adding:

- more ideas for songs and arrangements that YOU really like
- pieces that you notice elicit responses from others
- requests from customers, family and friends—definitely worth the trouble to find.

I know what kind of music interests ME, but I have no idea what to learn, or where to find what others like. Only once in a while do I pick a winner. How do I find winning songs?

If you are on the lookout for appealing new songs, these steps may help:

1. Ask different types of people for their favorite performers.
2. Scan arts sections in newspapers for the latest in shows, movies and award-winning songs.
3. Learn songs requested by your customers.
4. Keep abreast of TV shows and special presentations.
5. Notice the canned music in stores.
6. Observe TV commercials. (Their writers have already researched the music that people like.)
7. Look for party tapes in party stores.

Also, don't be concerned if you learn a new song and it falls on its face. Some ideas were simply meant to be tried.

My strength is jazz tunes. People love my "standards" repertoire, but I am playing too much of the same style, offering almost nothing to "Top 40 s" customers. They are into music I don't know anything about.

Listen to radio stations that attract younger generations. Select the pieces that will work on your instrument. You will also notice all the remakes of songs with which are familiar to you.

Young people do not necessarily want to hear "hits". They do enjoy hearing melodies they recognize from movies or TV as well as the melody lines of well known classical selections.

Save a song:

 Keep in your repertoire at least one new piece from every major gig. Enter the song into your repertoire notebook and use it!

> We have a list of songs we'd like you to play.

Some of the flashiest jewels in your repertoire will come from specific pieces people ask you to prepare.

How much time should I spend learning requests?

Only you can judge the time you can devote to looking for or learning the new repertoire. It's like starting any other business—you must invest some extra time when you're getting started.

What should I say when wedding couples or party hosts ask me to provide numerous requests?

You could tell people who hire you that you have access to X number of libraries (one is your own home library) and if you can't find some of the requests, you'll let your employers know early on so they can provide you with the music or a tape. Be sure they are aware of the music you DO play—it may suffice. If a host gives you an unusually long list:

DO make an effort to supply an appropriate number of the requests.
DON'T feel pressured to find them all.
DO notify the host well in advance what you can supply.
DO speak enthusiastically and cheerfully, stating the positive first.

Note the following conversation between a musician and bride:

Quartet leader: Hi, Ms. Bride? I found three pieces composed by Handel for your prelude music!

Bride: Oh, that's fine.

Leader: But I wasn't able to locate the last one on your list.

Bride: Don't bother, we'll have the D.J. take care of it.

Requests are supposed to HELP you add to your repertoire. How would you respond in the following situation:

You are booked to play for a community club in two weeks. The secretary calls, informs you that the theme of the gathering is autumn and asks you to play "Autumn Relieves" and other songs with September or autumn in them. You grew up in California and never learned much about autumn.

Musician 1: They have a lot of nerve. They're trying to take advantage of me.

Musician 2: Hey, that's a famous song. I can add it to my permanent repertoire. My neighbor might have the CD, or I could pick the melody out.

This chapter has discussed in detail the importance of learning new songs. But often what is needed is your *old* repertoire played with a *new*, fresh approach. Ask yourself, what does this room need? If it is March, the need may be to lighten up and inject some spring into the atmosphere. Imagine you are in a Jamaican band, wearing a straw hat and playing steel drums. Add some calypso rhythms to songs you already know, and you will feel like you have a whole new repertoire.

Styles to play

Let's talk about styles. If you are strictly a rock artist, jazz musician or classical player, you may want to become fluent in several instruments to increase your gig potential. The alternative is to learn many styles of music, and have more variety to offer audiences.

If I learn a bunch of styles, will people call me a "Jack of all trades and master at none?"

There is no reason that a musician can't become a "master" at several different styles of music, similar to the way a linguist can effectively speak many languages.

Musical categories

When you book yourself or your ensemble for receptions and parties, people will ask, "What kind of music do you play?" Which of the following categories does your repertoire include?

- pop
- rock
- jazz
- classical
- Top 40
- country
- soul
- folk/ethnic
- gospel
- Broadway

Each of these styles listed is very broad. For example, jazz includes ragtime, standards, blues and boogie. If a customer asks for rock, have him specify specific performers, or even decades of the rock styles he prefers. Many customers don't think in terms of styles, but of favorite songs or music for dancing.

Speaking of styles, are you beginning to develop your own style of playing?

What's my own style? I just play a bunch of pieces.

170

style, *n.*
1. distinction.
2. character.
3. originality

Help! I'm just trying to get the notes right!

Sonia was a wind player auditioning for an all-female jazz combo. When a band member asked her what kind of music she played, her answer was, "Oh, everything." The band member replied, "Oh, mishmash." Sonia did not bother to be offended by this: she knew that versatility is a skill in itself and can result in more work.

Improvising

I can't improvise. I don't know anything about jazz.

Who said improvising was limited to jazz?

improvise, *v.*
1. to compose, or compose and perform, on the spur of the moment.
2. to use the tools at hand, usually to fulfill an unforeseen and immediate need.

Hey, this definition doesn't say anything about jazz!

According to the dictionary, improvising is not limited to playing jazz. Many situations arise that require a musician to improvise.

*   Your trio is entertaining at a luncheon. You are all seated, waiting to resume playing after hearing a short awards presentation. Suddenly, the lights are lowered and a procession of waiters strides in, each carrying a grand flaming dessert. The head waiter motions for you to play something appropriate.

*   A student disc jockey at a campus radio station asks you to play fillers on the guitar to enhance his show.

*   You bring a synthesizer to an improvisational comedy group rehearsal. They need mood music for skits and filler for scene changes, and you are willing to give it a try.

*   You are entertaining for a children's party, and the small guests need music to play musical chairs. To challenge yourself, you try composing on the spot, rather than playing songs they know.

*   You are accompanying a school play for which bowing music is needed. You "make do with the tools at hand," playing snippets of the

score to match each main character.

While improvising in these situations may now seem scary, when the need to improvise appears, you'll use your skills and repertoire in a new way.

Playing by ear

I need written music. I can't play by ear.

Perhaps you have never really tried it and are unaware of your ability.

Notes from A. Gigger

having completed a music degree, i only played from da notes.	i took a gig that required lots of current hits. hits I know
the sheet music was expensive and had very complex rhythms.	guess what? listening to the recording eliminated having to count. CD
one day i received a special request tune for that evening. cassette in hand, i timidly picked out the melody.	from then on, it was me and my ear.

When you learn a song by ear, you end up appreciating *something* about it, whether you intended to or not. A musician often faces a mental block because a he does not WANT to appreciate a particular song. Perhaps it is below the level of music he has spent many years practicing. But the challenge of learning by listening when the job requires it will definitely make him a better musician and improve his ear for the music he prefers.

Learning a piece by ear from a tape

1. Start with a simple piece.

2. LISTEN AND DETERMINE WHAT IS APPEALING ABOUT THE SONG. You will learn it more easily if you like something in it. For example, you might say, "I like the unexpected harmonies—the ones that I can't define," or "It's relaxed and happy."

3. After listening several times, take a break. When you return to the song, you will notice more details. Listen beyond the notes and search again for qualities that appeal to you, such as the singer's free and easy style, or the meaningful words.

4. Listen to specific parts that make up the song. Begin with the words. Then, listen to the melody and sing along with it. What is the form of the piece? Is it verse-chorus-verse? Examine the bass, which may be difficult to hear.

5. Use your instrument to discover the key. (The key is usually the bass note that starts and finishes the song.)

6. Go back and play the first melodic phrase. Immediately stop the tape and sing it aloud. Then play the phrase on your instrument. You may need to replay the recorded phrase many times.

7. Continue this listening/singing/playing pattern until you finish the melody.

8. Continue if your instrument requires chords and filler. **The following text and notation provide basic theory for a reader who has had little formal instruction or one who needs to utilize it more effectively.** These are some commonly played keys, with the most important chords labeled I, IV and V.

Key of C Major

Key of F Major

Key of G major

Using these triads as a model, establish the I, IV and V chords in your key. Example: if your key is B flat, the I, IV and V chords will be B flat, E flat and F.

9. Listen to the piece several more times, this time focusing on the bass line. Hum along with the bass—hearing the bass will help you find the chords.

10. Try to play the correct chords along with the tape, stopping and repeating whenever a correction needs to be made. Continue until you can play chords along with the whole song.

11. It is important to take breaks and allow the work to "sink in." You will come back hearing the harmonies more clearly.

12. Listen to the piece once more adding melody to the chords.

13. To add filler and other details, repeat the same phrase-by-phrase method.

Why should I bother to sing the words if I am an instrumentalist?

You will learn the meaning of the song and play with more expression. Singing helps memorization, too.

I can't hear the bass at all, even when I turn it up.

Yes, the bass is very hard to hear sometimes. You will become more aware of the bass with practice.

There was one chord in the piece that wasn't included in the triads.

Yes, and that is probably the most interesting harmony in the piece. The more you understand chord structure, the better your ear playing will be. Jazz or theory lessons can give you this knowledge.

NOTATION

You may choose to immediately write down what you hear.

Listening and writing it down

1. Follow the first three steps of "Learning a piece by ear."

176

2. Using staff paper, write out the words, spacing so that the notes can fit above them.

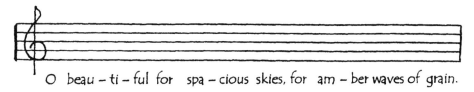

O beau – ti – ful for spa – cious skies, for am – ber waves of grain.

3. Listening again, fill in the bar lines.

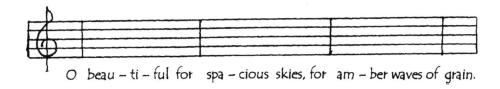

O beau – ti – ful for spa – cious skies, for am – ber waves of grain.

4. Write the melody notes without note values. At first, you will probably need your instrument to do this. However, aim to notate without your instrument—this will improve your musical skills.

O beau – ti – ful for spa – cious skies, for am – ber waves of grain.

Add note values and harmonies.

O beau – ti – ful for spa – cious skies, for am – ber waves of grain.

Whether you are listening for melody, rhythm or harmony, concentrate on ONE ELEMENT AT A TIME.

Why should I put forth this effort when I can buy a computer

177

program that will do it for me?

Computer programs are useful when you are working under time constraints, but they will not improve your musical skills for this task. Learning to play and notate by ear (even while you're away from your instrument) will enable you to transpose on the job. You'll also be able to try tunes you've never played before, thus impressing and providing better service to your customers.

Once you become proficient at notation, this skill can become an additional source of income. Many amateur songwriters with no musical training pay others to put their songs on paper. Have these songwriters sing and record their original songs for you, then work from the recordings.

Chapter Sixteen:
GIGS SEMINAR

We made it –
our last week
of Gigs 101.

I love
field trips.

Waaa! I'm missing my
Saturday cartoons!

Welcome to the First Annual Gigs Seminar. Musicians from many backgrounds have come to share their experiences and trade ideas. We'd like to extend a big "thank you" to all of our panelists and participants, amateurs and professionals alike. Enjoy your morning, musicians; your lunch ticket is underneath your name tag.

Meet the Panel

Coordinator: Good morning! Thanks to all who joined us today both our audience and our panel—Ed, Julio, Di, Lo and Al. In this session, we'll touch on many ways to improve in different musical fields. We'll also spend devote time to setting goals. Our five panelists all are involved with different types of performing. Let's begin by having each one share a few things about himself or herself. Ed, can we start with you?

Ed: Sure. I'm in my last year at State University, working on a double major in computer programming and piano performance. I started playing professionally in high school.

Coordinator: What did you do?

Ed: I played at a restaurant in Pittsburgh. Actually, it was a real dive and I played in the men's room.

Coordinator: Thanks, Ed. How about you, Julio?

Julio: Well, it was quite a drive to get here! My act right now is singing cowboy songs at a dude ranch. Each morning we have a trail ride breakfast, then I play guitar and sing in the evenings there. I also play with an R&B band.

Coordinator: Sound like a great job, if you like riding! Di, would you tell us about yourself?

Di: I'm a singer. I can also speak several languages and have been doing voiceovers in Polish and Russian on TV and radio. I teach music part-time in a public school, too.

Coordinator: Lo?

Lo: During the week, I'm at home with two small children. Five years ago

I started playing jazz flute with some friends, and it's turned into a combo that plays on weekends. We have a steady Sunday brunch job and work many Saturdays, too.

Coordinator: Finally, Al and I have known each other since we played in a high school rock band.

Al: That was 25 years ago. I keep busy with an orchestra and composing now.

Coordinator: Al is now the musical director of the Al Sans Orchestra, which a national magazine listed as one of the country's leading society orchestras. Now that we're all introduced, I'd like to ask everyone a question. What do you like about performing?

Julio: It's fun! You meet so many people and see how they live.

Di: It's sometimes glamorous: you dress up and receive tons of attention, which balances with the hours when you are only musical wallpaper.

Lo: Gigs are so civilized!

Coordinator: What do you mean by that?

Lo: I mean, it's a privilege to play music for even a part of my income.

Julio: Yeah, it IS a real satisfaction, especially being asked to play overtime because people are listening and don't want to leave.

Al: I just like entertaining. I like bringing out the music in other people.

Ed: I like it the most when people react and sing when I'm playing, or bring kids over to watch.

Coordinator: Well, we've got an enthusiastic panel here. Let's move on to the topic of Improvement.

Improvement

Coordinator: Let's talk! The question is, "How do YOU need to improve in your individual field?" What do you say, panel?

Al (orchestra leader): I want to be a more versatile player. I've played sax and clarinet all these years, but I'm practicing xylophone lately to become proficient in a new area. It's influenced my composition, too.

Lo (flutist): You're right; instrumentalists get more work if they can double up. I've found that a musician needs to be as versatile as possible.

Julio (guitarist): Especially for theatre and studio work.

Di (singer, music teacher): Versatility has gotten me several singing and playing jobs. I'm not a great pianist, but if a one-night job for a pianist/singer comes up, I can handle it.

Lo: Di, it's interesting how you utilize your skill at languages, too.

Di: It really fills a need, sometimes more than my singing in English does.

Ed (college piano major): I see what you're saying about versatility. I couldn't find any work playing piano solo last fall, but as soon as I teamed up with a string player, we were asked to play for two weddings on campus.

Coordinator: It sounds like versatility is the answer to getting more work. Back to improvement; Ed, what are you focusing on right now?

Ed: School! But for weekend work, I need to develop a bigger, more expansive sound on the piano. I need a huge, octave melody line and a powerful bass just to be heard when there's a crowd.

Di: How much technique are you doing?

Ed: My private teacher has given me a daily warm-up of scales and arpeggios.

Di: You're lucky to be working on heavy classical pieces in school. You can use that technique in your arrangements.

Lo: My gig needs more new tunes, and all of that sheet music is expensive!

Ed: I used to buy sheet music until I found out that I could learn by ear.

Al: I had a Master's degree before I discovered the same thing.

Di: It helps to take jazz lessons and learn more about theory and chord structure.

Lo: I don't know if this pertains to the subject of improving, but my combo needs a list of reliable substitutes. I had a student cancel two weeks before New Year's Eve. It's a disaster when they do that.

Di: If a person has to cancel, he should offer a sub, at least.

Al: If it's a constant problem, seek out more experienced musicians. Really, a musician's motto ought to be, "Go Anyway." If you're afraid to drive in the snow, go anyway. If someone calls you to sub and the pay is lousy but you haven't worked for two weeks, go anyway.

Ed: I agree about the subbing. You can learn a lot from sitting in someone else's seat for a night. It can lead to a steady job, too.

Coordinator: Julio, we haven't heard from you yet.

Julio: I feel like my ranch act is at a standstill. I don't think about improving; I just think about getting paid!

Coordinator: I see some hands up in our audience.

You don't get it. I have a day job.

I have 8 loads of laundry on Tuesdays.

I have Driver's Ed and baseball.

We don't have time to improve!

Coordinator: No time! How do you handle that problem, Al?

Al: I went through years of working various day jobs and gigging at night. But every one of the day jobs contributed in some way to my current business. Let's take a look at what you ARE doing. Are the challenges of your employment or lifestyle helping you improve in ANY areas?

Coordinator: Why don't we start a list?

PERSONAL QUALITIES
- concentration
- alertness
- endurance
- physical appearance

CUSTOMER SERVICE
- being open-minded and flexible
- happy attitude
- willingness to meet others' needs

WORK WITH FELLOW EMPLOYEES
- appreciation
- positive attitude
- communication skills

Al: Imagine a commercial musician with two hours a day to practice. After three years, his technique was flawless but he hadn't matured in any of the above skills.

Lo: He wouldn't be a balanced act. I had to take one year off from music each time I had a baby, but being a parent and later a part-time teacher helped me grow in many of those areas.

Al: Growth in any or all of these areas will give you more musical success, even if the success comes at a later date.

Coordinator: This discussion has made it clear that it's very important to focus on individual improvement, being versatile and making the most of whatever situation you're in. I think we all deserve a short break. Take 10 minutes, and we'll come back with the topic of Best Teachers.

Coordinator: Welcome back, everyone. We haven't moved too far from the topic of Improving. The new question for our panelists is this:

Besides actual persons, what have been your best music teachers?

Ed: First, I have to say that I have a great teacher at school who is helping me to prepare for my recital. But I would say that in playing commercial music, recordings are my best teachers because they're indispensable to learning new tunes.

Al: Self-critique is my best teacher. No one could possibly criticize my work as much as I do.

Di: I learn to entertain from watching live performances, good and bad. I learn about musical styles from recordings.

Ed: Speaking of bad, many accompanists have made me wince by not giving the soloist enough support in the bass. I've done it, too, but sitting through a performance like that is a painful music lesson.

185

Julio: The best lessons on rhythm I ever had were the drum and bugle corps performances every Fourth of July.

Di: Speaking of live performances, one that made a big impression on me was at a wedding reception. At the toast, one guest stood up and sang an old love song. She sang with such confidence that the song became one of my favorites to perform.

Lo: Any experience that helps you grow can improve your playing. Even events that take you away from your art for years, like an entirely different career, can give you a new appreciation and maturity when you do return to your music.

Coordinator: So far, our panel has nominated self-critique, recordings and live performances as candidates for Best Teachers. Can anyone in the audience add to the Best Teachers Besides Teachers list?

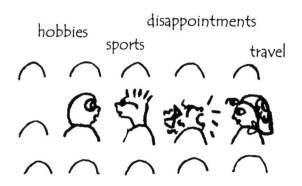

Coordinator: Wow! What a list! I think we're all in agreement that any experience that makes you grow can help your playing mature, too—even if not until a later date.

Coordinator: Audience and panelists, I have a treat for you. A. Gigger is here to read his winning entry in our Best Teachers essay competition.

For years, i wanted to learn a certain piece.

certain piece ♪ ♪

there was this technical part in it that i simply couldn't master. i was afraid of it!

i had this persistent urge to go to the video store and rent a fred astaire movie.

i watched one, taps, top hat and all.

in one song, the couple danced with the strength of athletes, flying around the floor in a frenzy.

the dance showed me how to play my piece! fred and ginger were the best teachers.

The End

Goal
Setting

Coordinator: I think we all discovered at our first recitals that the best way to improve is to have a goal.

Goal, *n.*
1. the end or final purpose.
2. the end which a person aims to reach or accomplish.

Coordinator: Panelists, would you mind sharing some of your musical career goals with us?

Ed: For now, I just want to play more, maybe in places around the university. Later, I want to teach and perform at the college level.

Di: I'd like to support myself entirely with my voice. Naturally, I want to make CDs and be a STAR.

Julio: I used to have big, big dreams of being famous with my band. We came close to some successes, but we argued so much that the group finally broke up. We just didn't have enough teamwork. Now, I just want to make a decent income and have a house and nice truck.

Lo: I want to stay in one location and have a large following. In the next few years, I want to improve my playing enough to do studio work. All of my work needs to fit in with raising a family.

Al: I'd like to keep up the orchestra bookings AND spend more time composing. Any other dreams, I keep to myself!

Coordinator: You've all mentioned long-range goals. Can you give us some ideas of how to work with goals in mind?

Al: Make a list of short-medium- and long-term goals. Short-term, or immediate goals, are what you have to accomplish for the next gig.

Di: Excuse me, Al, but I have to jump in and add that the best time to write a list of goals is immediately *after* a gig. Then you really know what you need to do!

Lo: But in reviewing even a rough gig, don't get bogged down with self-criticism. Acknowledge your improvement, too.

Al: I agree. Anyway, medium-range goals are what you need for projects in the next six months. Long-range goals include chiseling away at a recording you'd like to make in a year, or five years.

Ed: It's kind of like school—you start planning for finals in September.

Lo: Don't forget about wild and crazy dreams, too!

Di: This is a crazy but possible dream—I'd like to entertain in an amusement park, maybe for a summer. I know they hold auditions in the fall, so I'm planning for it now, by preparing my act and saving money to fly to Florida for an audition.

Coordinator: Let's take a look at the overhead screen. Our panelist Ed has provided us with a recent gig which seems to need some improvement. We're going to help him with his goal setting.

Ed: ... so that I can feel like a professional instead of a student.
This is a recent wedding reception that I played with friends at school. I felt like we were so amateur!

The reception music was too stiff. Loosen up!

The classical pieces had very amateur-sounding arrangements.

189

Throw away the pop books! Make a list of memorized pieces and have more fun!

Replace the sheets that look like your dog chewed them.

 At least the wedding was fine.

Coordinator: This is quite a gig, Ed, with plenty of comments. Panelists, what does Ed need to do now? How should he spend part of his practice time this week or this month?

Ed: My short-term goal is to write a list of my own repertoire to give to other musicians on the job.

Al: You can easily find authentic music to replace the bad arrangements. Try college libraries.

Di: For a medium-term goal, you can make a list of the songs your duo knows from memory and play them at the next gig.

Ed: Yes, the next wedding job is three months away. By then, I'll have neater, more organized books, too.

Coordinator: I see a hand up over there.

Making goals would have helped me in the past. I took composition and quit. I'm on my fourth voice teacher. I've dabbled in jingles, musical theatre and coaching, but I've never stayed with any one thing until it became any sort of success.

190

Julio: Why do you keep quitting?

It doesn't seem like quitting. One project just pushes me into a new one.

Di: Well, it sounds like you consistently work with music.

My question is, are my experiences considered failures?

Lo: How can anyone call something a failure if it's something you learned from? I would just call them experiences.

Di: Meeting smaller goals within each activity would have made you attain more successes. For example, you could have aimed for a yearly performance with each teacher, or completed one major composition and copyrighted it.

Al: It's good to have a goal and work until it is accomplished. But it's also good to have an experience that prepares you for something else.

Di: Or just makes life interesting.

sweet dreams

Perfect day. I went to the seminar and had a gig.

All I did today was go to a seminar and have one gig.

When I'm famous, Boomer will call me and...

2:00 a.m. rock.

Lo: Ed, with these short and medium goals met, you'll have more spontaneity and enjoyment.

Coordinator: Panelists, can any of you relate to the problem of a musician having so much work that she doesn't enjoy it anymore? What can you say to this case of gig burnout?

Ed: Nothing. I'm not even close to that.

Al: I say, cheer up! Your misery is pushing you to progress. Get out your motives and review what you are aiming for.

Ed: Motives?

Motive, *n.*
1. Some inner drive, impulse or intention that causes a person to act in a certain way.

Lo: We all mentioned material goals before, but there have to be deeper ones than to simply stay interested and excited. Sometimes I ask myself, "Do my goals go beyond advancing me, myself and I?" Motives need to be continually polished.

Al: I constantly ask myself WHY I am pursuing this or that project. The burned-out musician can start with that question, and prepare for a new and higher step.

Coordinator: This ends today's seminar. Thank you all for coming and contributing. Finally, to all musicians present: **THANK YOU FOR SHARING YOUR MUSIC!**

Chapter Seventeen:
DA CAPO AL FINE

Well, class, Gigs 101 has come to an end: we have covered many, many topics in the field of musical performance. You are ready to play your music in a more professional way. Now, go out and gig, gig, gig!

194

GIGS 101

Index

Order Form

Send *Gigs* to a friend!

E-mail orders: amazon.com (credit card payment)
Or mail this form with check or money order to:

Benny Publishing
9403 Lincolnwood Drive
Skokie, IL 60203

MAIL ORDER FORM

Please send me ___ copies of *GIGS: A Beginner's Guide to Playing Music Jobs*. Enclosed is a check or money order for $18.95 per copy plus $4.00 shipping and handling for the first copy and $2.00 for each additional copy.

Amount enclosed_____
Name_____
Address_____
City/State/Zip_____

Contact Benny Publishing for discounts on bulk orders.